72-0

Date Due

MAY 2 2 1985
DEC 3 1 19

HABIT
AND
HABITAT

OTHER BOOKS BY
ROBERT THEOBALD

ROBERT THEOBALD

HABIT
AND
HABITAT

PRENTICE-HALL, INC.

Englewood Cliffs, New Jersey

Graph entitled "World Population and Energy
Production" from *The Future of the Future* by
John McHale, published by George Braziller,
Inc. Reprinted with the permission of the pub-
lisher. Copyright © 1969 by John McHale.

Graph entitled "World Energy Consumption
in the next Century—a possible pattern" from
The Next Hundred Years by Harrison Brown,
James Bonner and John Weir. Copyright ©
1957 by The Viking Press, Inc. Reprinted by
permission of The Viking Press, Inc.

Three charts entitled "Percentage of World
Food Imports Going to the United States 1963–
1965"; "Percentage of World Food Exports Go-
ing to Western Europe, 1963–1965"; and "Water
Required for Daily Per Capita Food Production,
United States and India" reprinted with permis-
sion of The Macmillan Company from *Too
Many: A Study of the Earth's Biological Limi-
tations* by Georg Borgstrom. Copyright © by
Georg Borgstrom, 1969.

CONTENTS

ACKNOWLEDGMENTS

This book is one result of the overall learning process which I have experienced during my lifetime. The ideas expressed here have grown out of discussion with many people, some of whom I have met only once or infrequently and others with whom I have been in continuous contact. In particular, this volume results from the efforts of my wife, J. M. Scott, who developed much of the fundamental thinking.

R. T.

PREFACE

Man is unique. This statement has been made so often—
and so incorrectly—that we have lost sight of the few areas
where it is profoundly true. In particular, we fail to remember that man is the only species which has developed the
means to force his habitat into patterns which he desires.
He has used ever-greater power to enable him to do what he
wants to do and prevent those patterns which he finds
undesirable.

All other species work within the existing habitat. Their
success or failure depends upon their ability to adapt to the
conditions in which they find themselves. Their survival
depends upon a complex, interrelated ecosystem of which they
form a small part and over which they have very limited
control.

Man alone has tried to deny his relationship to the total
ecosystem of which he forms part by continuously ignoring
and cutting off feedback which he finds undesirable. He has
developed the habit of seeing his habitat as totally flexible
according to his own wishes and desires.

Americans, in particular, have developed exploitative habits.
They have traditionally believed that they are reclaiming land
from the wilderness—rather than receiving a gift prepared by

God or nature. The habit of giving thanks for the cooperation of God or nature has essentially vanished in the United States. The European harvest festival which recognized the place of God's grace in bountiful crops was transformed into the American Thanksgiving—an increasingly secular feast which boasts of man's supremacy.

Although man's pride in his own potential developed farthest in the United States, it is a basic industrial-era trait. In the nineteenth century, Lewis Carroll, a British mathematician, wrote about the Mad Hatter's Tea Party where everybody moved round to the next place at the table when he had soiled his own dishes. Carroll was drawing attention to the fact that Western man saw no need to clean up after his activities.

The recent environmental movement grows, of course, out of this recognition that we have failed to take responsibility for the world in which we live. The failure of the environment movement to develop a coherent diagnosis of the problem to guide decision making explains, in part, the fragmentation of analysis through which we are presently moving. Environmental groups are trying to deal with various symptoms of the environmental crisis rather than with the central problem.

Some groups are primarily concerned with the rapid growth of population—they are therefore concentrating on finding means to reduce the rate of increase in numbers. Other groups believe that the problem stems essentially from the abuse of technology—they propose to solve the difficulty by limiting or abolishing technology. Still other groups see the difficulties as arising primarily from increasing consumption per head —they are striving to create a consumers' revolt against shoddy and valueless goods.

The thesis of this book is that the causes of the environmental crisis lie far deeper. The habits we have developed during the industrial era toward our habitat are now so inappropriate that only a fundamental change in thought and action patterns will make any real difference to man's future. If this argument is correct, the relative failure of the environment movement is due to the fact that it deals with symptoms rather than causes.

How does one change fundamental habits and institutions rather than superficial behavior patterns? Arnold Toynbee, the British historian, has argued that cultures have always failed to carry out such a task in the past. Assuming the validity of this statement, we are confronted with an ahistorical situation, which must be tackled using new techniques.

These new techniques must be developed for *all* our patterns of behavior, including the way we write books. The purpose of socioeconomic books today is, in almost all cases, to propagandize for a particular set of policies. This volume, on the other hand, aims to help people to perceive the ways in which they presently think, to prove their irrelevance in existing conditions, and to suggest alternatives. If this task is to be achieved, it is necessary to present the same issue from several points of view. The reader who is accustomed to fully structured arguments may find this approach difficult—a full explanation of its necessity is set out in Chapter 7, which deals with what we have understood in recent years about learning processes. (This discussion was necessarily placed relatively late in the volume because considerable groundwork needed to be laid before it can be easily understood.)

In addition, two chapters are largely nonverbal. They attempt to develop ideas in new ways. These chapters will not, of course, be helpful to all readers, but we have discovered that they are valuable for those who do learn in non-linear ways.

One final issue must be clearly raised before entering upon the central argument. This book is written from the point of view of the abundance regions of the world. The scarcity regions necessarily see things very differently. U Thant, Secretary-General of the United Nations, stated the situation clearly in his introduction to *The Challenge of a Decade*:

> Mankind must decide during the seventies whether it is willing to change in order to take advantage of its new potentials. Continuation of present patterns of behav-

ior for a further decade will create a situation in which our very survival will be uncertain.

We must rid ourselves of the poisons which result from continued colonialism and racism. These divisive factors limit cooperation. They also prevent us from creating the true global partnership required for success in the process of development.

Three immediate steps are essential. We must commit ourselves to using our rapidly increasing technological knowledge to feed, clothe and shelter every human being on this earth. We must commit ourselves to eliminating war as a method of settling international disputes, thus freeing the resources required for the development process. We must commit ourselves to maintaining the viability of this planet whose very survival is now threatened by pollution.

If we are to succeed, we must recognize that not only are these three commitments necessary but that their priorities are seen differently by the rich and the poor. The poor are naturally primarily concerned with their immediate needs for food, clothing and shelter. The rich, on the other hand, have achieved their immediate physical needs and they are therefore freed to be concerned about the impact of environmental pollution.

The raising of the environmental issue in the United States has already proved profoundly divisive: the poor and minority groups have felt that it lessened the chances of dealing realistically with their existing problems. If this reaction should become worldwide, it could tear the world apart. The chances for the survival of the world would then be negligible.

PART 1 THE END OF THE INDUSTRIAL ERA

CHAPTER 1 WHAT FUTURE FOR THE ENVIRONMENT MOVEMENT?

Despite its apparent successes, the environment movement in the United States may still die. If it is to survive and grow it must fulfill its promise to educate the public so that it has the knowledge to act to avert our ever-deepening ecological crisis.

The environment movement grew in the second half of 1969 and the winter of 1970. It began to decay in the spring of 1970. The various strands of action and protest which had come to typify the environment movement culminated on Earth Day, April 22, 1970, and then had nowhere vital to go. It is certainly true that the American invasion of Cambodia on April 30, 1970, deflected attention from the environment movement. However, the main reason for the failure of the environment movement up to this date is that it has tried to handle complex issues in a superficial manner. It is caught up in exactly the same pathologies of thought and action that caused the ecological crisis in the first place.

The issues raised by the environment movement are nevertheless real and immediate. They came to public awareness because of a wide range of concurrent trends which, perceived together, produced a new and more realistic awareness of mankind's situation. This new awareness was accompanied by a new mode of thinking, which is changing the world in which we live. This book will reexamine the nature of this new awareness and the new mode of thinking which could enable us to create a world in which we could live humanly.

A new awareness

During the sixties, a large number of people were developing a new perception of the world and of their ability to affect the world. People began to see connections between processes which they had previously considered unrelated. For instance, it became clear that the presence of oil wells near a resort town and beach in Southern California could imperil the economy of the town and the health of its flora and fauna. It remained, however, difficult to determine the implications of this insight, for the economy of the town still depended on tourists who used cars which used gasoline which came from oil which came from wells.

Western industrial-era societies have typically thought in terms of first-order connections: we knew that cars had to have gasoline in order to run. In the late sixties, we began to perceive second-order connections: that cars running on gasoline place poison in the air we breathe. Now we are beginning to see third-order connections: unless we drive automobiles, we cannot get to work to receive a paycheck. The next step is to recognize that the whole economy of the developed countries depends at this point on an ever-increasing consumption of cars and gasoline and other goods and services. So long as present socioeconomic systems continue, therefore, it is essential to build more highways and drill more offshore wells and pour more poison into the air we breathe.

Man, his social order, and his environment are interdependent: worsening conditions in the social order generate worsening conditions in the environment. The corollary is also true. Worsening conditions in the environment create worsening conditions in the social order. The combination of a worsening environment and a worsening social order today threaten man's survival. The present threat to man's survival cannot be significantly lessened without fundamental changes in our thinking and social systems.

Many changes of this nature are already taking place, but their interlinked importance has not yet been recognized. Indeed the environment movement could only grow so fast because other related patterns were developing concurrently. For example, management theory has stressed for many years that a manager who delegates responsibility and keeps communication lines open is more effective than one who attempts to control his subordinates. The resulting management style led some businessmen to see the inherent interdependency of their enterprise with the society in which they do business: they are discovering second- and third-order connections between the way they act and the world around them.

Similarly, those concerned with education have been discovering that teachers and students must work together. Education cannot be effective if it is perceived as a one-way communication during which the teacher pours knowledge into the student like a pitcher pouring water into a glass. Effective educational processes require that the student teach the teacher at the same time the teacher informs the student of what he has previously learned. This new style of learning inevitably leads to the recognition of second- and third-order connections in the education process.

Underlying these concurrent trends is a shift in our basic theoretical understandings. The physical sciences have come to see that the physical universe operates as a field of force with reciprocity, connections, and interdependence between its constituent parts—rather than as a clock, as had been assumed in the industrial era. The physicist Heisenberg proved that the observer stance is impossible: the act of observation necessarily affects the situation which is being observed. This is even truer in the social sphere: acts of observation and the methods used to describe that observation necessarily affect the situation. Conversely, the situation itself determines the degrees of freedom available to the observer. A person affects and is affected by events even when he is trying only to observe them. We always act in a network of interdependent processes.

The new style of thinking which developed concurrently with the environment movement can be described in terms of the growing ability to perceive reciprocity, connections, and interdependencies. This process can be defined as "systemic thinking": a person thinks systemically when he perceives connections, interdependencies, and reciprocal relationships in the real world in which he lives.

Systemic thinking is presently replacing linear thinking, which was the dominant mode during the two hundred years of the industrial era. The linear thinking of the industrial era required the setting of immediate goals: people then acted to achieve them regardless of the secondary and tertiary consequences of their actions. For instance, a chemical company might decide to market a new insecticide in order to increase its profit. Only too often negative evidence about the effect of the insecticide on human tissue and on the chemical/biological composition of the earth was ignored or suppressed because it would reduce or prevent sales and thus decrease profitability.

New patterns of behavior

At the same time as many people were creating a new awareness of their relationship with the environment, they were also developing new ways of acting. New ways of acting are, in fact, inevitable whenever thought processes alter. Unfortunately, the significance of the emerging patterns of behavior is still generally misunderstood.

In the second half of the fifties, the general mood in America was lethargic and directionless. During the sixties, however, America began to move. Some of the energy was used to create new patterns of behavior. A larger proportion of it was used in attempts to destroy old patterns of behavior which had dominated the West for the last one hundred years.

One significant, and early, attempt to build new cultural patterns was the hippie movement of the middle and late sixties. Hippies consciously aimed to create behavior patterns which would reflect and encourage the new awareness of reality which they had gained. For instance, they perceived that people can be gentle with one another: so they dressed in soft fabrics and wore flowers. They understood that the suburbs, from which most of them came, tended to isolate people from one another: so they tried to create situations in which individuals would have emotional support.

Unfortunately, however, the total society misunderstood hippies so badly and overpublicized them so heavily that the valid messages of the hippie movement were destroyed, and a "plastic" movement developed in its place. This attracted many who had no idea of the discipline the hippie movement necessarily implied.

Concurrently with these initiatives by hippies, other groups in American society were creating their own patterns of behavior. People in minority groups began to examine the uniqueness of their traditions and to define themselves in terms of their uniquenesses instead of in terms of dominant middle-class mores. For instance, Indians rediscovered their traditions and saw them as valuable and well-suited to the ways they wanted to live: they began to demand the right to choose their own situations and conditions. Similarly, blacks grew to believe that their route to personal and group development was by demonstrating their uniqueness and building a community spirit around their own values and ways of life. Mexicans, Puerto Ricans, and other Spanish-speaking groups came to believe the same things about their communities. All of these groups have increasingly argued that a full life requires the acceptance and development of the values and patterns of behavior which come from one's tradition. The desire to choose one's own life-style also lies behind the Women's Liberation Movement and behind the concerns of the old and the young for greater personal meaning.

Substantially new behavior patterns were also developing in business. Following the social upheavals in the mid-sixties, businessmen perceived that the location of their facilities, the qualifications demanded by their personnel departments, and the effect of their operations on the environment all influenced their ability to do business in a community. The old rhetoric about the "responsibility businessmen have for their community" is being taken increasingly seriously.

During the sixties, many people gained a new awareness of themselves and their environment. The new awarenesses often appeared divergent, and some people changed more rapidly than others. Nevertheless, the sixties were a time of fundamental change in our style of thinking, and this change is irreversible. If we are willing to take the necessary time and make the necessary effort, the changes which have already taken place can indeed form the basis for creating a more human society.

New awareness of responsibility

The changes of the sixties have *begun* to reverse the thinking and action of the previous century. During this period, Western man came to believe that he could do *anything* he wanted to do. He moved away from the thinking of the agricultural period when man's successes were seen as based on his cooperation with nature.

Today we are learning that we cannot do everything we wish. The finiteness of the planet sets limits on our power, as does the fact that the world is interdependent and connected. Desired goals have secondary and tertiary consequences which can often be undesirable. We can achieve any goal which is critically important to us, but our very success can set up consequences which we would have wished to avoid.

The automobile is a classic demonstration of this point. Most Americans have cars to provide mobility but their real mobility is limited by the fact that *other* Americans also have cars. In addition, the pollution from the cars increases upkeep costs of gardens, homes, and businesses, worsens health, and causes premature death.

We are being forced back to the question which Western man has forgotten. Man may be able to do *anything he considers vital,* but he cannot do *everything he wishes.* Given man's rapidly growing power, we must ask ourselves what it is important to do, which range of choices we wish to develop.

This question is gaining increasing acceptance as *the* relevant question of the seventies. However, we shall only deal successfully with it if we recognize that it has emerged from a new level of awareness. This question of what should be done cannot be asked, or answered, by those who think linearly. In order to handle this question we must learn to think systemically. The nature of the issues inherent in the question "What *should* be done?" differ profoundly from those inherent in the question "What can be done?"

Ten years ago the United States did not ask whether we *should* send men to the moon: it was assumed that the trip would be desirable *because* it was possible. It is only recently that we are really challenging the goals implicit in this and other similar decisions. We are recognizing that we can no longer assume that everything which is technologically feasible is humanly desirable.

Systemic thinking is therefore being forced upon society. More and more people are considering secondary and tertiary consequences of actions. Fundamental changes in patterns of perception are occurring throughout the country. This book will study the causes of these new patterns of perception and explain why they are essential. It will also suggest some of the steps which must be taken if new perceptions, new awarenesses, new patterns of behavior, and new cultural patterns are to develop. In effect, the volume will develop the rationale for systemic thinking and show how the society might develop if we use systemic thinking intelligently.

Such an effort is profoundly subversive. We are accustomed to thinking linearly. Our whole society is based on linear patterns of thought. Our very patterns of communication are determined by this linearity. The shift toward systemic thinking, which this book presents as essential, has a profoundly disorienting effect. However, nothing less than a complete restructuring around the insights accorded by systemic thinking will suffice to meet the enormous problems and possibilities which mankind has now identified.

Systemic thinking is, of course, in its infancy. Its uses have, in consequence, so far been dangerously partial. For example, conservationists use systemic thinking to point out the threat of oil wells and industrial wastes, but most of them remain unwilling to face the systemic need for fundamental change in life-styles if we are to limit the need for oil wells and the production of industrial wastes. Businessmen are coming to understand that they have a fundamental responsibility for the quality of life in the communities in which they produce and sell, but they generally remain unaware of how their constant pressures to increase consumption undermine their efforts to improve the human condition.

An overview of systemic thinking

Systemic thinking requires a fundamental change in our patterns of perception, understanding, and action: in one sense the whole of this book is devoted to reaching the point where the individual begins to understand the patterns required if systemic thinking is to replace linear thinking. Fundamental shifts in pattern are never comprehended until they have been repeatedly worked with.

Nevertheless it appears essential to introduce the basic concepts behind system thinking at this point. The central concept is that the present perceptions and action patterns of any living being or group of living beings are based on and constrained by past patterns of behavior, that they can be changed if there is an understanding of desirable alternative ways of acting but that any effective change will necessarily be evolutionary, rather than revolutionary, in character.

Living beings or groups of living beings have their present

limitations and potentials built into them by their genetic inheritance and their cultural characteristics. The mix of long-run genetic patterns and shorter-run cultural patterns varies with the nature of living beings—the behavior of human beings, with which this book is primarily concerned, is more largely controlled by short-run cultural characteristics than other species.

How can we change the perceptions and cultural patterns of human beings so that we can preserve the earth? The fundamental reality is that change is always situational: the methods of appealing to individual human beings and groups of human beings will depend on their own hopes and fears. The ability of any individual or group to perceive the relevance of the environmental issue at any point in time will depend on the cultural attitudes with which they grew up and their situation: it is for this reason that the poor are relatively uninterested in this range of topics. At a recent environmental conference, it was argued by inner-city dwellers that the society should be more interested in the elimination of rats than in the preservation of eagles. If the appropriate attitudes for environmental concern do not presently exist, they must be developed *before* action to maintain and save the environment can reasonably be expected.

Intelligent system change depends on a society effectively carrying through certain steps. The society must perceive the directions in which it is presently moving and recognize that it will continue to move in these directions in the absence of new constraints or new ideas. Social trends can be compared to billiard balls: they continue in the same directions unless they are constrained by a cushion or another billiard ball.

In today's world, however, when thought and action patterns are changing so rapidly, social trends will inevitably clash with each other. There will be massive turbulence in the seventies as long-established trends come into conflict and those involved in the conflicts fail to understand the nature of the disagreements in which they are involved.

Extended continuance of this turbulence will shake America and the world apart.

The only way to avoid this turbulence is for mankind to understand clearly what is actually happening and to accept fundamentally new styles of behavior appropriate to our growing ecological understanding. We need new dreams which take account of man's growing potentials. We must create the dreams which will move people to change present trends in directions which will permit man's survival.

Understanding the past and developing dreams of the future are only the preparatory tasks toward discovering the evolutionary steps required to mesh the past with the necessary and desirable future. We are forced to move in evolutionary ways to achieve fundamental change, because there is no way to pick up a total system and move it bodily into another mind-set and world view. Attempts to achieve change by revolutionary means may alter the names of institutions and the faces within them: they will not bring about fundamental changes in the way the culture works. This is the fundamental lesson of the French and Russian revolutions.

A good analogy to our present societal requirements is provided by the recent demolition and reconstruction of Penn Station in New York. It was necessary to destroy the old building and create the new one *without* stopping railroad traffic. A detailed plan had to be developed to achieve this task. Similarly, we must build the values and institutions required for the future without destroying the values and institutions presently ensuring mankind's survival: industrial-era values and institutions must continue to operate until they have been effectively replaced.

The societal task is clearly more difficult than the rebuilding of the railroad station for two major reasons. First, the degree of complexity of the task is far greater. Second, there is no cohesion of purpose. While those involved in the demolition and reconstruction of Penn Station agreed on the value of the task, there is as yet no agreement even on the need for societal reconstruction—let alone on the directions in which the reconstruction should proceed.

Those who wish to alter societies must therefore learn high-level communication skills so that the problems forcing changes and the possibilities which could emerge from change are translated into languages and concepts that those who must change can understand. The process of change can only be understood and accepted if there is true participation within it: if the process of change is not understood and accepted, frustration will develop and violence will inevitably follow.

We are confronted with a situation in which we must creatively respond to forces which were created in the past. Man's survival depends on his increasing his decision-making capacity as greatly as he has increased his productive power.

This book is written for those who would like to be involved in understanding why we need new institutional styles and in finding out how to create them. If the reader believes that we already possess all the solutions to the environmental crisis and that our only problem is that we are failing to apply them, this book will be of little interest to him. The volume is written for the growing number of people who believe that a new, systemic mode of thinking must be developed if we are to solve the ecological crisis.

Because this book is designed to help the reader develop systemic modes of thinking, most people will gain most from the book if they move with its flow rather than skip and examine those chapters which seem most immediately interesting. The concepts necessary to read later chapters are developed in the earlier ones.

CHAPTER 2 *THE ORGANIZATION OF THE SUPERINDUSTRIAL SOCIETY*

The United States is profoundly ambivalent about revolution. She is proud of her birth in conflict and struggle. Today, however, many Americans are deeply dismayed because a significant part of the total population believes that further fundamental change is necessary.

The American culture has its present form because the values of immigrants were altered from those which they possessed when they arrived in the country to a belief in the possibility of progress. Nevertheless, it is also Americans who are most likely to use the cliché "You can't change human nature."

Americans do not understand the degree to which their values changed during the industrial revolution. Most Americans would agree that their institutions and values did alter during the industrial revolution. However, few Americans would agree about the extent or nature of the changes which occurred.

How extensive were the changes? Two examples can be given which are representative. First, it was agreed in the late Middle Ages that poverty was due to the failure of the society rather than to the failure of the individual. Giving to the poor was therefore a fundamental obligation of the rich:

charity carried a very different connotation. Today the American culture acts as though success results from the efforts of the individual—or sometimes the total family. The poor are normally perceived as idle and shiftless members of the society.

Second, there have been profound shifts in the relation of the individual to information. In the Middle Ages, information was considered to belong to God and the Church. It was not until the eighteenth century that the concept of copyrights and patents developed. These entitled the individual to an exclusive, if temporary, right to the results of his work. Today the idea that the individual should benefit financially from his writing or invention is deeply imbedded in the culture.

These are two of the more obvious illustrations of changes in institutions and values during the industrial revolution. For a fuller understanding of the meaning of these changes we must examine several issues in more detail. This chapter will examine developments in economics, the threat of a neo-Luddite revolt, and the use of the bureaucratic style. In addition, the chapter will examine the way in which the linear mode came to dominate the thinking of economics, the language and actions of individuals, and the organization of the society.

Economic theory before the Great Depression

There can be no doubt that the formal discipline of economics is today the most linear of all the social sciences. Its methods of analysis are limited. They exclude all factors except the narrowly economic. Economists deal with abstractions such as the Gross National Product and the unemployment rate. The attitudes of individuals, institutions, and nations enter economics by the back door: for example, through studies of consumer confidence and discussions of the reasons why certain percentages of the labor force choose to look for work and to stay at home.

How did economics get to the point where it felt justified

in excluding so large a part of human experience and values and concentrating on so little? Why did economists decide to examine *means* to achieve economic growth without considering the *consequences* of a drive for maximum economic growth on social and ecological patterns? Why did the branch of economics concerned with the welfare of human beings (welfare economics) die out in the period following the Second World War?

It is certain that Adam Smith, on whose work modern economics is based, would be shocked by recent developments. Smith was concerned with the ways in which the value structure (world view) of a country determined its ability to produce and distribute goods and services. His view of economics placed the attitudes and activities of the individual, which are largely determined by his culture, at the center of the economic process.

Looking backward, we can see that Smith created two critical insights. The first insight was that the amount of production depended on the division of labor. The more specialized the worker, the greater the amount of production which could be achieved. He showed that as activities become more specialized, the worker would become more skilled and the amount he could produce would rise. Different workers could then carry out complementary tasks and would produce more than if each worker carried out all the tasks for himself.

Smith's first insight is clearly a special case of ecological reality. Environments are most likely to be stable—and productive—if they contain a large number of different organisms. The wider the range of organisms, the more complete the use of available resources: e.g., light, heat, water, etc. Each organism, well suited to its ecological niche, draws on a different portion of the available resources. The complex pattern of interrelationships and feedback which are inevitable when many organisms coexist in a given ecological niche make it more probable that the total ecological system can survive extremes of climate and other similar shocks, although some organisms may die out. The greater the complexity of an ecological system, the more unlikely it is that any one organism will come to dominate the whole system and the greater the long-run stability of the system.

Smith's statement was relevant when he wrote it. It has, however, become incorrect and dangerous, because it has been developed linearly over the past two hundred years. For example, the idea of specialization has been carried to extremes. Specialization has become counterproductive in many areas, because men are complex organisms and they have unfavorable psychological and physiological reactions when compelled to cut off too wide a range of their physical and mental capacities. In addition, economists have lost sight of the wider ecological truth in order to concentrate on economic matters alone. Today, economists encourage specialization in the economic sphere without considering that continued specialization can limit and destroy many of the inherited biological specializations of other organisms which provide the framework in which man himself can safely specialize.

Smith's second critical insight was that the process of creating specialized skills in the labor force was limited by the extent of the market. In other words, the extent to which it is economical to produce ecofacts—goods and services—in specialized ways depends on the number of people who will want them after they have been produced. If the demand is limited, it may be better for a single individual to produce an ecofact rather than for many people to gain the specialized skills required for "efficient" production. In the absence of sufficient demand, efficient production results in an excess of available ecofacts.

Smith's second insight is also a special case of an ecological reality. The wider the range of conditions available within a given environment, the larger the range of specialized organisms which can be supported within it. Once again, however, the special economic form in which Adam Smith stated his theorem has led to misinterpretation. The broader ecological meaning has again been lost, and economists have pro-claimed the possibility of the indefinite extension of markets for ecofacts.

The high point in relating economic and ecological think-ing followed Smith. Malthus, writing early in the nineteenth century, demonstrated that there are limitations on popula-tion growth and economic production. He argued that the potential rate of *population* increase was greater than the potential rate of increase in *production* needed to support the increasing population. He argued, therefore, that either the human race would learn to control the rate of population increase or numbers would be controlled by natural (ecolog-ical) limitations.

Malthus' statement, of course, is no more than a tautology in ecological terms: populations are always limited by the resources available to them, and resources are finite. The fascinating question we must answer is why economists found it increasingly possible and desirable to ignore the les-son taught by Malthus. As we have seen, one answer is to be found in the growing dominance of linear thinking. The very fact that Western societies have succeeded in keeping production rising more rapidly than population over 150–200 years, led economists and other commentators to argue that the process of economic growth could continue indefinitely.

Economists have been struggling ever since Malthus to eliminate any need for system thinking. They have sought to introduce total linearity into economics and to get rid of all aspects of the subject which could prevent rigorous, linear analysis. In the 1870's a school of economists, generally called the neoclassicists, were believed by their economic col-leagues to have accomplished the task. The assumptions which they created and from which they worked were as follows:

> 1. Human beings are "economic men" ruled entirely by economic motivations. They do not consider social or psychological satisfactions.

2. All firms are small. No firm can use power to distort the market for its own advantage.

3. There are no labor unions. Workers are not able to combine to attain power to raise wages.

4. There is no government intervention in the economy. The power of government is not used to alter prices of ecofacts or to distort wages and salaries.

5. There is correct information available so that people can carry out those activities which are most profitable to them.

6. There are no fundamental changes in conditions —economic, technical, social, etc.—over time.

Until the Great Depression of the thirties, the mainstream of economics worked within these assumptions and used them as a basis for two activities. First, economists tried to discover what the *exact* theoretical consequences would be *if* neoclassical assumptions *were* fulfilled. Second, economists tried to manipulate the real economy so that it would accord as closely as possible with the theoretical assumptions developed by the neoclassicists. The fact that the conditions postulated by the neoclassicists could obviously never be achieved in practice—and that the validity of the policy conclusions derived from the model was therefore uncertain— worried an ever-smaller proportion of the economics profession.

The social sciences have hidden their fundamental assumption patterns for so long that we have forgotten that it is impossible for conclusions to be any better than the assumptions and data on which they are based. We would not be impressed with a strategy for world trade which was based on the assumption that the world was flat. The dangers of basing economic policy on an incorrect set of assumptions are equally serious.

The consequences of false assumptions were, in fact, dramatically demonstrated during the 1930's. The gap between theory and achievable reality was a large part of the cause of the Great Depression. In accordance with neoclassical assumptions, the economists of the late nineteenth and early twentieth centuries tried to hold down the power of *all* groups to distort the operation of the market system. However, the success of their actions varied with different groups. They were reasonably successful in their efforts with both the unions and the government. On the other hand, the measures which were passed to control business—such as antitrust laws—were largely ineffective. By 1929 the power of the corporations was so great, compared to other economic institutions, that major imbalances had developed. These imbalances made a depression inevitable.

The rationale for economic growth

Although it is obvious in retrospect that America's basic problem in the thirties was the excessive power of corporations and the distortions in income distribution caused by their power, this reality was not clear even to those economists who were most influential in conceiving new policies during this period.

John Maynard Keynes, the great British economist, was primarily responsible for the development of the ideas which have dominated Western economic thought and action during the last thirty-five years. Keynes proved that it was possible for machines and equipment to remain unused even though individuals had large unsatisfied wants. He argued that countries could only ensure demand for all the ecofacts (goods and services) which could be produced if there were fundamental changes in economic and financial structures.

The initial strong theoretical opposition to this point of view had been overcome by the end of the Second World War. Policy, however, did not change as rapidly as theory. Indeed, the last barriers to the full operation of Keynesian policy were only breached in the sixties. Nevertheless, in the immediate postwar years, all Western countries adopted policies designed to ensure that there would be full employment. This policy was a fundamental departure from past patterns when recessions were considered normal.

The new policy arose because people believed that all the

ecofacts that could be produced should be consumed and that the appropriate way to ensure the right to consumption was to provide jobs for all. This policy built a drive for maximum rates of economic growth into Western economies.

The goal of maximum economic growth is based on an unprovable value judgment: that it is desirable for a society to produce as much as it is technically able to turn out. The logic of this value judgment is as follows. It is perceived that possible production will not be consumed unless people possess, and are willing to spend, the resources required to purchase available ecofacts. It is believed that people should normally acquire resources to purchase ecofacts through holding jobs which produce incomes. It follows, therefore, that the desire to consume must always rise as fast as the capacity to produce, for otherwise sufficient jobs will not be available. It also follows inevitably that the society must be so organized that each worker can gain sufficient skills to be able to hold a job which will provide an adequate income.

As a society we are committed today to full employment. This commitment to full employment makes necessary continuous pressures for increased consumption and continuous retraining. As a result of these societal requirements, the relative power position of corporations, the unions, and government has changed dramatically. In effect, the very acceptance of Keynesian beliefs has changed Western beliefs and social structures so fundamentally that Keynesian analysis has itself been made invalid. The further continuance of policies based on Keynesian policies has become impossible because of the changes in beliefs and social structures.

In order to implement Keynes' ideas, the dominant position of corporations had to be effectively challenged and a rough parity of power established among corporations, unions, and governments. This change was completed by the fifties. Today, unions and corporations—and to a considerable extent governments—all have an interest in growth at any price. The drive of these groups toward continued growth leads to the danger of permanent and growing inflation, for there are no effective penalties for implementing excessive rises in prices and wages.

It has, of course, always been in the interest of firms and workers to push up prices and wages as rapidly as possible. All groups, however, were restrained from excessive upward pressures by fear of pricing themselves out of the market and also by the belief that a general recession was possible if the general price level rose too rapidly. The commitment of Western governments to continued growth has removed the real danger from both these threats—inflation is inevitable until the inappropriateness of Keynesian policies in today's changed conditions is recognized.

WE CAN NO LONGER ACHIEVE BOTH ECONOMIC GROWTH AND STABLE PRICES. Given this reality, we must decide whether to tolerate inflation or unemployment. One or the other—or both—is inevitable so long as we try to solve economic problem/possibilities on the basis of Keynesian assumptions and policies.

Our difficult economic situation is made more serious by the political developments resulting from Keynesian policies. The rough parity of power which was achieved in the fifties among the unions, the corporations, and the government led to a situation in which decision making was based on countervailing power. Different groups tried to influence policy in directions which favored their objectives. Each group tended to adopt a no-holds-barred approach, with the result that ever-increasing amounts of pressure were applied to persons in a position to formulate policy.

As a consequence of this new ordering of society, the individual became unable to influence policies which affected his life. Since policy was determined by competing power blocs, the thinking of individuals was increasingly pushed out of view. Since the individual could not be effectively involved, he came to feel powerless and devalued.

A social order based on countervailing power is antidemocratic. When policy is controlled by competing power blocs, the thinking of individuals is obscured. Democracy is not possible within the linear order of the industrial era: it is only possible when society is organized systemically.

The abundance of ecofacts

It is now urgent that we replace the economic theory on which present policy is based. To do this we must reexamine whether we should continue to be committed to maximum economic growth.

The fundamental justification for policies designed to maximize economic growth is that people always need more ecofacts than they already possess in order to live fuller lives. This is the unprovable value judgment on which the industrial era is based.

It is, of course, obvious that people who can purchase too little food, clothing, and shelter for minimum levels of decency will benefit from more. In the scarcity regions of the world, it is clear that additional ecofacts will be of value. However, beyond the physiological needs for survival, definitions of desired quantities of ecofacts depend on cultural values and philosophical concepts. Many cultures have been based on the belief that one should reduce one's physical needs to the level of available possibilities rather than strive to raise one's capacity to produce in order to meet increasing desires to consume. The desire for a high standard of living and large quantities of ecofacts are, therefore, culturally conditioned. Wants for ecofacts do not grow automatically. It is our industrial-era culture which has developed specialized means to increase the wants of individuals. Today economists often claim that people have unlimited wants for ecofacts. This statement contradicts a basic thesis of economics: that there is declining value to anything as one possesses more of it. If this basic economic theory is correct, people should come to value time for enjoyment of ecofacts more than the ability to acquire further ecofacts as they become richer. The consumption of ecofacts would level off as the need for ecofacts is satisfied. There is very considerable evidence that people and cultures do react in this way. For example, Americans are increasingly angered by the amount of selling pressure in their culture. Instead of being easily turned on to new products by advertisements, there is now a strong resistance to advertising. For example, there are now attempts to ban commercials on children's shows. Furthermore, there are growing efforts to remove billboards from roads and highways.

A shift in values is taking place. The culture is moving away from its previous commitment to a growing consumption of ecofacts and is beginning to place an emphasis on other goals. It is therefore increasingly unreasonable and unrealistic for those managing the nation's affairs to act as though there were still a cultural commitment to unlimited economic growth. The present movement away from an unlimited commitment to growth has a startling implication: it becomes progressively less possible to continue to guarantee full employment. Our present method of distributing income in the United States is therefore becoming less functional as rates of consumption grow less rapidly.

We have a choice: we must either continue to force increasing consumption so as to provide enough jobs to perpetuate full employment, or, if we no longer consider such a system desirable or possible, we must change fundamentally our methods of distributing income.

The growth of automation and cybernation

In reality, no present or proposed set of policies can ensure full employment in either rich or poor countries during the seventies. The progress of automation and cybernation is now so rapid that computers and computer-aided machines are less costly than men in many jobs. This reality has so far been largely disguised by government training programs and government pressure to hire workers who are not competent. It has also been disguised by the hoarding of personnel during the Vietnam war. It now seems certain that a new pattern will emerge in the first half of the seventies. Growing unemployment rates among the highly skilled and well educated, as well as among other workers, are the first indicators of this trend.

When the costs and benefits of employing workers are examined, not only must one consider the wage costs, but one must also calculate the value of the time required to organize the work of less-skilled workers. Those who organize others obviously have alternate uses for their time. As the number of people who are truly competent to work with computers and system theory is very small, and as such people may well be taken off this work to organize the activities of others, the real cost of using incompetent workers is very high both for the employer and for the society. The overall economic effect of employing many types of workers today is negative. More would be produced if many people were fired because they waste the time of others more competent than themselves. In addition, there is always the chance of errors, and in today's complex organizations, errors may have serious consequences.

In addition, it is time to recognize that government training and retraining programs have mainly helped those who would have been able to find a job for themselves if the government had *not* been involved. Government programs are effective when the cream of the unemployed is skimmed, but they have never reached the hard-core unemployable.

As these realities have been understood, there has been a growing demand that governments should serve as "employer of last resort" and hire all those who cannot find conventional jobs. The idea of using the government as the employer of last resort ignores the fact that the government is no more capable of employing the unemployable usefully than is private industry. The whole proposal is based on a faulty parallel with the thirties. In the thirties, people had skills but no jobs. In the seventies, the unemployed do not have the required skills: in particular, the unemployed lack the capacity to compete with already developed machine systems.

Keynes' assumptions are today so unrealistic that the conclusions derived from them are *necessarily* wrong. Keynes wrote for conditions which no longer prevail: "We take as given the existing skill and quantity of available labor, the existing quality and quantity of available equipment, the existing technique. This does not mean that we assume these facts to be constant, but merely that in this place and context, we are not considering or taking into account the effect and consequences of changes in them." We cannot expect to deal with the unemployability crisis until we cease to base our policies on obsolete assumptions.

One of the steps toward reorganizing our thinking is to recognize that present methods of calculating Gross National Product assume that all outputs are positive. The locks which are needed to protect people from a growing crime rate count as part of the Gross National Product: so do the expenses of commuting to work. The costs of cleaning drapes and carpets, clothes and children, cars and buildings all add to stated production. Equally seriously, the destruction of a forest by pollution will not appear in calculations of the Gross National Product at all unless money is spent to save the trees—then any expenses required to correct the costs of past behavior are shown as positive.

In this context, we can examine another bias in the calculation of Gross National Product. The value of the work done by a woman in her own home does not enter the Gross National Product. On the other hand, if she goes out to work and *at the same time* hires somebody to look after her baby, the amount earned at her job *and* the amount paid to the baby-sitter both enter the Gross National Product. Once again, therefore, calculations of GNP overstate benefits and understate costs.

Official economic data show that the economic state of the world is improving. However, calculations based on reasonable assumptions about costs and benefits might lead to an opposite conclusion.

The neo-Luddite revolt

The growing understanding of the difference between official economic statistics and reality is one of the major factors changing patterns of behavior in America. One of the most critical new behavior patterns is the neo-Luddite revolt which is developing with great rapidity in the United States at the present time.

In the early nineteenth century, a group of people in Britain called Luddites became dissatisfied with the developing industrial system under which they were living. They saw the source of the problem as the growing productive power of the machine. They therefore tried to smash machines which they feared would put them out of jobs and thus destroy their community life-styles.

Similar forces are developing today to cause a neo-Luddite revolt. Workers and management alike are coming to see that they are likely to lose their jobs because of the new technologies. The fear engendered by this recognition will increase rapidly in the future as it becomes clear that automation and cybernation do actually provide the potential for producing more ecofacts with less labor. In addition, marketives—all those engaged in selling ecofacts at a profit—have discovered that they have been paying people who do not contribute significantly. Computers are now being used to analyze efficiency and to discover who is not contributing to production. It therefore seems highly improbable that the excessive staffing which led to full employment in the sixties will be permitted to develop again.

The destabilizing impact of automation and cybernation will increase rapidly in the future because it was consistently denied throughout the sixties. During the last decade Americans should have faced the fact that the goal of full employment had become obsolete and needed to be replaced by the goal of full *un*employment. We shall now pay for our failure to recognize that the goal of full employment is obsolete. A substantial proportion of the population is committed to a backlash against what they consider to be the cause of the unemployment: the technological infrastructure. The actions of the neo-Luddites will range from simple efforts to delay changes which would increase the effectiveness of marketives —a collective word for all groups producing ecofacts in order to gain a profit—to deliberate acts of sabotage.

One example of this trend is the fact that middle management in many firms has been unwilling to cooperate fully in efforts to introduce computers for fear of an unfavorable impact on their careers. Another trend was demonstrated in a recent *Fortune* story which proved that the boredom and frustration of automobile assembly-line workers was causing them deliberately to act in ways which would make automobiles less satisfactory and even dangerous.

The range, and possible impact, of the neo-Luddite revolt is increased by the fact that both individuals and the society feel that they are being victimized by machines. Recently, Johnny Carson had a guest on his late-night show who had shot with a pistol a vending machine which had failed on many occasions to provide change. The incident, of course, was unimportant in itself. The significant aspect was that both Johnny Carson and the audience sympathized with the man who had shot the machine rather than with the owner of the machine who had brought the man to court for damaging property.

The propaganda of many ecology groups has added to the neo-Luddite attitude. These groups often see technology as the major cause of the breakdown in the ecosphere. Some ecology groups have dramatized their hatred for technology by purchasing cars and then breaking them up with sledgehammers. As this attitude spreads, it tends to diminish the chances for gains in productivity which could be made at this time.

Unfortunately, the work of Jacques Ellul and Lewis Mumford is also being used to feed the neo-Luddite revolt. When he wrote *The Technological Society* in the early forties in French, Ellul was attempting to draw attention to the real effects of technology on Western societies. His work was analytical and should have been used as a stimulus to rethink Western values and social patterns entirely. Initially, his work was ignored. Now, however, it has been discovered, but not for the reasons or by the people for whom it was originally intended. Today, Ellul's work is being used not as analysis leading to rethinking and creation but as a rationale for a policy of destruction and violence. *The Technological Society* is being read as indictment rather than as analysis. Lewis Mumford's work is also being misused in similar ways.

The neo-Luddite revolt also rests, in part, on the belief that it is desirable to break the present society down because its life-style is unattractive or intolerable. It is argued, correctly, that American society would collapse if its production, transportation, and communication marketives could be crippled.

Neo-Luddites do not realize, however, that their approach works against their stated goal of diminishing the dominance of machines and the linear mode of thinking. As we saw in the previous chapter, social systems inevitably continue to evolve in the same direction unless they are attracted in a different direction by clearly defined alternative routes. In order to create new patterns of attraction, it is necessary that those who have already perceived the need for change create attractive options for the culture. Any breakdown in communication and transportation nets necessarily hampers such an effort. The neo-Luddite revolt, therefore, has the ironic consequence of making a total cultural/ecological collapse *more* probable.

In addition, a neo-Luddite revolt in the seventies is highly immoral if one considers its worldwide impact. We have few years left to start the process by which we shall move the necessary resources into the scarcity regions of the world. While it is certainly true that we do need new concepts if the abundance regions are to help rather than damage the scarcity regions when providing aid, it is also true that we cannot provide significant resources to the scarcity regions unless we have effective production, communication, and transportation nets in the abundance regions.

The incompatibility of bureaucracies and communities

Neoclassical and Keynesian economic assumptions made it possible to reduce economic phenomena to measurable data. Economics was the first of the social sciences to move toward the respectability of a hard science. The other social sciences pressed hard behind.

In the process of moving toward measurable data, patterns of acceptable language changed. We reached a point where the worst term of opprobrium that could be leveled at an idea was that it was value loaded and not objective. Our striving for objectivity originated in industrial-era organizations. Later, however, the same striving for objectivity spread into the whole society. The growing passion for objectivity necessarily dissolved community values and relationships, for these were based on subjective factors, and their validity failed to stand up under the solvent of objectivity.

This dissolving force of objectivity is today being challenged as human groups, both small and large, strive to reestablish personal contact. There has been a particular drive to re-create community living, but major difficulties exist. First, community traditions are no longer real to many, and those to whom they are real—that is, many older people—often share too little with the young to be able to teach them. In many cases, the very concept of community as an entity which provides freedom by developing responsibilities has been lost. Even more seriously, it is now clear that when a community does succeed in developing its own life-style, it threatens present bureaucratic institutions which, by nature, are inimical to individuality and novelty. It becomes impossible for the new communities to communicate with bureaucratic institutions successfully.

Let us look at a dramatic example of the collision of communities which are trying to develop their own life-styles with the bureaucratic organizations which presently form the social order in Western societies. Such a collision occurred in the Ocean Hill–Brownsville section of New York. This community, which is predominately black, became concerned with creating types of education which would be suitable for the children in the school district. At the end of the 1967–68 school year, the community asserted the right to fire certain teachers, on the grounds that they had not taught the community's children in ways which the community felt were appropriate.

The labor unions representing the teachers were immediately up in arms. They argued that due process had not been accorded and that the teachers had not violated any of the requirements for teaching in such a way as to justify firing them. The New York City educational bureaucracy was also hostile, for it perceived that if each school district claimed the right to hire and fire on the basis of its own procedures and criteria, there would be "chaos" in the organizational structures which they had to control.

There were long and bitter negotiations among Ocean Hill–Brownsville, the teachers, and the city educational bureaucracy. Agreement after agreement appeared to have been reached, but each agreement fell apart when applied in practice. In the end, Mayor Lindsay, the labor union, and the city educational bureaucracy held a meeting at which Ocean Hill–Brownsville community representatives were not present. This meeting imposed a settlement which effectively destroyed the style the community had been trying to develop.

It is still generally assumed by commentators that the failure of the community and the bureaucracies to reach agreement was due to an unwillingness on the part of the community to negotiate imaginatively and in good faith. In reality, however, the collision arose as a consequence of forcing together two incompatible world views. We must therefore examine why bureaucracies and communities are incompatible.

The industrial age, like all functioning systems, is necessarily based on a specific authority system. The existence of an authority system is a minimum requirement for the survival of any human group or society. Indeed, animals also use authority systems to order their lives. For example, many species operate with a leader of the pack who holds his position so long as his accumulated guile and his declining strength permit him to do so. When he can be bested by another animal, he is replaced. The authority system of many human societies is very similar: a leader retains his position so long as he can prevent another person from seizing power.

As human societies have become more complex, those in power have been surrounded with rationalizations and screens. These make it increasingly difficult to replace an incompetent leader with a truly competent one. For example, in modern Western democracies, the electorate has the power to replace the "ins" with the "outs." However, the political system works in such a way that the essential characteristics and policies of the "ins" and the "outs" are usually very similar.

The degree of flexibility in human systems has declined as they grow more complex, because organizations were required to enforce the will of the ruler and his laws. In order to do this efficiently, bureaucracies came into existence. Bureaucracies established and enforced rules and regulations which were designed to control more and more of the situations in which an individual might find himself.

It was Max Weber who developed the theory of bureaucracies to its fullest extent and, by so doing, helped it to reach its practical full flower. He showed that a successful bureaucracy must create a set of rules which will permit all individual cases to be neatly classified. If the scheme of classification is effective, there is no need for individual decision making. All possible situations are thought through beforehand and the steps laid out which should be taken in each situation. The ideal goal of a bureaucracy is to ensure complete objective justice by removing the human element and by ensuring that each individual, in an exactly similar situation, is treated in exactly the same way.

For this to be possible, it is necessary to try to invent a

totally logical, objective mode of communication. This objective mode must have all traces of subjectivity removed. In this book the objective, logical mode of communication will be called INTER. INTER is the impersonal, sterile language which is familiar to everyone who has dealt with a bureaucracy. The theory of bureaucracy is based on the assumption that INTER should make it possible for several interviewers to see the same client or to consider the same situation, and to reach the same conclusion about the appropriate course of action.

This theory was, of course, always invalid. It was invalid because there can be no way, even when a maximum effort is made, to exclude subjective factors from communication. Some interviewers will elicit more data from a client than others. Some interviewers will be antagonized by a client, and others will not. Some interviewers will know the law better than others and will be able to use it to benefit or damage the client according to their attitude.

In addition, present-day bureaucracies function increasingly badly because the rate of change is so great that bureaucratic categories cannot be expected to remain relevant over extended periods. Bureaucracies find it extremely difficult to change their goals even when it is clear that they are already counterproductive. Their style of organization makes them change resistant.

It is now possible to perceive clearly the reason for the collision between the community of Ocean Hill–Brownsville and the bureaucracies which opposed it. The bureaucracies had set up objective organizational patterns which were necessarily disrupted by the subjective community styles being developed by Ocean Hill–Brownsville. These new community styles emphasized that the level and pattern of interpersonal contact among teacher, student, and administrator were critical in evaluating the effectiveness of the teacher. The subjectivity of Ocean Hill–Brownsville and the objectivity of the bureaucracies could not coexist. The two groups had incompatible world views. When forced together, either the community or the bureaucracies would inevitably be destroyed.

The mutual incomprehension and attacks between those representing the two styles were inevitable. In addition, there was and is no available way of resolving this and similar disputes. The legal and quasi-legal structures of the industrial era are based on the same objective world view as the bureaucracies. Court cases or arbitration will therefore *inevitably* favor the bureaucracy rather than the community.

Our present institutional structures are designed to arbitrate between people who hold different goals but who see the world in fundamentally similar ways. The movement toward community, which requires systemic thinking, brings into existence a totally new situation. Those thinking bureaucratically and those believing in community hold two world views which clash. Neither world view sees the other as valid.

Bureaucracies, our only presently accepted form of organization, are based on the machine metaphor of the industrial era. It is therefore essential that we understand their modes of operation and their weaknesses if we are to be able to move into the communications era. The next chapter will cover this subject.

The industrial revolution was a huge success—in its own terms. In a relatively short period of time, enormous amounts of energy were harnessed and channeled to increase production and the available quantity of ecofacts. The success of the industrial revolution stemmed from the consistency and vigor with which bureaucratic linear thinking was applied: linear thinking effectively permits societies to concentrate on limited goals and to ignore secondary and tertiary connections.

The industrial revolution was possible because of the invention of machinery. The machine, in turn, was the product and embodiment of linear thinking. The machine was, par excellence, a manifestation of linear thinking. It was inevitable, therefore, that the machine would be perceived as the chief metaphor of the industrial era.

Indeed, the machine was used so widely as a metaphor that people gradually forgot that it was only a metaphor. Gradually people came to think of themselves and the world as a machine. For example, in the eighteenth century, the school of philosophy known as the Deists stated explicitly that God was a watchmaker and the world, the product of his craftsmanship, was a magnificent watch. The machine became a metaphor for the world, and the mechanic became a metaphor for the world's God.

Later the assembly line, developed by Henry Ford, came to symbolize the way things should be done: quickly, easily, and massively. Aldous Huxley perceived the reverence accorded the assembly line and suggested in his book *Brave New World* that events in coming centuries would be dated in terms of "After Ford." Society was also perceived as a machine. Today, therefore, many of those controlling large organizations still believe that the whole society can and should function as a machine operates.

The industrial era has spread the same basic mode to all parts of society: education, religion, business, law. The application of linear thinking and the machine metaphor to Western society is now virtually complete. Basically, Western societies perceive no other mode than the linear mode and no other organization than the bureaucratic. The machine metaphor is so widely accepted that it passes unnoticed. This conformity to one style of thinking and one style of organization ensures that all institutions in the United States, and indeed the West, operate on essentially the same ground rules.

Can this apparently extreme statement be justified? The following paragraphs will suggest some indicators.

Executives and persons with certain general skills move between companies and jobs with relative ease. Executives with chemical companies accept positions with electronics firms. A lawyer can become a government bureaucrat, and a professor can become an administrator. An executive with one voluntary organization will move to another in a different field or accept an appointment at a university. More startlingly, churches actively seek men with skills in business, law, and medicine to occupy positions of responsibility in the Church. Church structures are organized bureaucratically in the same way as secular institutions. The churches therefore can use secular skills without any basic change in style.

The parallelism of Church organization with secular

organization goes deeper. The churches' indicators of success are the same as those of the total society. Both churches and businesses count the number of people who obtain their products and the amount people are willing to pay for them. As a result, the churches must operate like other industrial-era institutions for the style of organization used by an institution constrains its goals.

Similarly, the helping professions—medicine, education, law—have come to use profitability as the main criterion of success. Increasingly people in these professions see themselves as engaged in businesses where their clients can be defined as malfunctioning machines: their goal is to get them back into efficient operation.

Another indication of our conformity to one style of thinking is the language we use. Listen to the repetition of the machine metaphor in these colloquial expressions:

Let's run this proposal through the mill.

The news media act as a conveyor belt for government propaganda.

The economy has built up a head of steam; let some steam out of it.

Toss that idea into the hopper.

That meeting was like going through a grinder.

Step on the gas and get moving.

Run him out on a rail.

This thing runs like clockwork.

He engineered the victory.

He's a big wheel.

That man is just a cog in the wheel.

Be careful or he'll steamroller you.

You want to throw a monkey wrench into the works?

The dominance of linear thinking and the machine metaphor enabled us to blind ourselves to almost all aspects of our culture except the economic. It is only now that we are learning that the success of the industrial era was bought at an extraordinary price. The price we had to pay was a loss of awareness of those realities such as beauty, love, and reciprocity which can only be perceived when one thinks in wholes or gestalts. By concentrating on one goal and refusing to look at the secondary and tertiary consequences of our actions, we lost the ability to perceive connections between ourselves and the environment. We lost the ability to think systemically.

> The improvement in city conditions by the general adoption of the motor car can hardly be overestimated.
>
> Streets clean, dustless, and odorless, with light rubber-tired vehicles moving swiftly and noiselessly over their smooth expanse, would eliminate a greater part of the nervousness, distraction and strain of modern metropolitan life.
>
> —*Scientific American*
> July, 1899

The success of the industrial era in creating machines and understanding the need for linear thinking was not dangerous in itself. If the new knowledge had been limited to appropriate areas, it would have been very valuable. The danger developed as people spread the machine metaphor and linear thinking over the entire society and came to believe that everything—even people—should operate as a machine operates. This spreading of the machine metaphor made it impossible to think intelligently about systems which cannot effectively be described in machine terms: e.g., organisms, human beings, societies, and ecological systems.

The extensive depredation of ecological systems in the name of economic growth did not occur because industrialists hated natural beauty and wanted to deny pleasure to other people. Rather, these depredations occurred because industrialists and the society as a whole were unable to perceive that economic growth would inevitably destroy ecosystems. Dominant western thought patterns were in terms of "economic progress," "growth," and "manifest destiny."

The systemic abuse of human beings resulted from similar blind spots. Sweat shops, child labor, pittance wages, and concomitant waves of robbery, extortion, murder, and every other violence were typical of the early industrial era. An apt name developed for people who benefited most from this system: robber barons. The abuses described by Charles Dickens and other critics of the industrial era were real and extensive. They derived inevitably from the style of the industrial era, which required the setting of a goal, and subsequent action to accomplish it by eliminating anything or anybody which might conceivably prevent the achievement of the goal. Brutality to those within the system was therefore inevitable. This explains in large part why Rap Brown, the black leader, argued that "violence is as American as cherry pie."

Continued dominance by linear thinking and the machine metaphor would make us incapable of handling our real problems and possibilities. Linear thinking cuts us off from perceiving what we are doing to ourselves and our environment. Industrial societies are profoundly blind to the full consequences of their actions. Linear, bureaucratic organizations inevitably think in terms of problems rather than possibilities. They use a style of thinking which is incapable of developing the potentialities of human beings, societies, and ecological systems.

Industrial societies today are experiencing the inevitable consequences of the attempt to treat people and ecological systems as if they were machines. Institutions are given little respect today because they do not function in the best interests of individuals or the society. Bureaucratic institutions only act in terms of legalisms, precedents, and old norms. We cannot emerge from our present critical situation until we cease to see our problems as being predominantly caused by individuals who fail to obey these legalisms and precedents. We must come to understand that our major problems result from the fact that our present institutions are incapable of facilitating the best interests of individuals and the society.

We are suffering from a malfunctioning society—amondie—
rather than malfunctioning individuals—anomie.

The incompetence of our institutions

What are the inherent weaknesses which make linear
organizations incapable of making the kind of decisions
which are necessary today? Why are organizations designed
on the basis of the machine metaphor totally inadequate to
carry through the systemic rethinking which is now essential?
As we examine these questions, we must be aware of a deep
illogicality in the present situation. Our major institutions
are still linear and bureaucratic, but at the same time 'most of
the population perceives the need for greater personal freedom. Even those who call most loudly for "law and order"
wish it to be applied to others, while they want their own
areas of freedom increased. We are truly caught between two
eras, one dead, the other struggling to be born. Our societal
commitment is to the control systems of the industrial era.
However, our personal commitment is to a more open society.
This situation is new. It is also hopeful if we can come to
understand it. The situation will remain dangerous until we
become aware of its implications.

We therefore need to look at seven inherent weaknesses
of linear organizations:

They can only receive information they are designed to
receive.

They can only make linear decisions: they only extend
existing decisions.

They are easily overloaded and underloaded.

They are susceptible to the Peter Principle.

They are only capable of reproducing their type.

They tend not to pass unfavorable information up or down
the chain.

They are only capable of controlling people who wish to be
controlled.

LINEAR ORGANIZATIONS CAN ONLY RECEIVE INFORMATION
THEY ARE DESIGNED TO RECEIVE. A linear organization can

only receive information which fits its classifications. It is limited by its classification scheme. Let us look at some examples.

Within the present legal system, cases can only be tried within existing laws. Lawyers and judges must therefore force cases into existing categories. Given the pace of change, many cases today involve issues and conditions which existing laws do not satisfactorily cover. These cases must be tried not in their own terms but in terms which do not apply to them. Similarly, the mass media inevitably use their own classifications for events they report. These classifications usually bear little resemblance to the realities of the events which are reported. Again, doctors are taught to look for certain patterns of ill health. As doctors become increasingly specialized, one man knows only a limited number of patterns. If a doctor does not know the patterns of ill health of a given patient, he cannot help the patient.

Police also have certain limited classifications they use in making arrests. For instance, several women and a man traveling on the Long Island Railroad at night in 1969 became disgusted with the filth and undependability of the railroad. In protest, they decided not to surrender their tickets. They were hauled in for "theft of services" and treated like criminals. They were intimately searched, locked up without communication, and forced through various indignities. The police would not listen to their story: they were forced into the legal classification scheme "theft of services."

A linear organization, such as a bureaucracy, can only handle information for which it has a classification. Bureaucracies confronted with input patterns for which they have no classification possess only two choices: either they ignore the input, or they force the different information to conform to their existing classification scheme. In both cases, the new, often valuable, information is lost to the bureaucracy. It is this depersonalizing or dehumanizing act of a bureaucracy, in order to make individual cases conform to its formalized classes of information, which is commonly called Kafkaesque, after Franz Kafka who wrote novels depicting the patterns of bureaucracies. It is important to recognize, however, that this behavior is inherent in bureaucracies and not due to the evil of individuals within them. It is senseless to become angry at bureaucrats, because the real problem is in the nature of the bureaucratic style itself.

When the incident involving passengers on the Long Island Railroad came to the attention of the mass media, it was widely called Kafkaesque. It was recognized as Kafkaesque because those who got caught in the situation were normally excluded from interactions of this type with the police. We fail to recognize, however, that Kafkaesque activity is carried on every day by social workers, credit bureaus, automobile mechanics, ministers, university professors, and the media itself. The inevitable Kafkaesque act stems from the linear way we have organized ourselves. Our way of structuring knowledge and ways of acting, in fact, cuts across the inherent needs of situations in which we find ourselves.

For example, people who are discussed in the mass media often wonder how the information on the screen or the page came out the way it did. During his campaign for the Presidency, Senator Barry Goldwater stated that the media failed to understand and convey what he was saying. Many people who lose elections make this sort of statement. If they were candid, the winners would say the same thing. Similarly, every President has complained that the media fail to convey the messages he wishes to get across.

The categories used by the media to define relevant information *differ* from those used by the President. The President is interested in holding the country together, bringing about essential changes, and conveying information, often in careful tones, to citizens at home and diplomats abroad. The media are interested in news. They require novelty as a minimum and usually also the presence of some type of crisis.

The classes of information used by *both* the President and the media are inherently incapable of expressing the realities of today's world. The categories employed by the media and the President do not include many of the categories relevant to a person living in poverty or to a minority leader, to the young or to women. The categories of both the media and the President are derived from the industrial era.

Bureaucracies often make one small *theoretical* concession to the fact that people and ecological systems do not fit their classifications. They use the idea that there are "shades of gray." When something has "shades of gray" this means that it fits two or more classifications rather than a single one. Part of the problem is thus solved rhetorically, but nothing significant has been altered. Bureaucracies may discuss "shades of gray" but decisions and actions must still be clear-cut, "black and white." The idea of "shades of gray" has a theoretical but not an actual value. It is a device to make people who are affected by the bureaucratic style believe that the bureaucracy at least tried to understand them.

For example, a clerk in a credit bureau often finds that an individual's performance in paying bills should not bring him a negative rating, but neither does his performance entitle him to a positive rating. The individual's performance falls in those gray areas which lie between classifications. However, in the end, he is rated either positive or negative, and therefore his true performance is not communicated.

In summary, linear organizations are limited by the fact that their reception channels restrict the amount and type of information they can receive.

There is a second way in which linear organizations are limited by their classification schemes. They are extremely vulnerable to strong input approaching them at a point where they lack regular reception channels. They are vulnerable, that is, to information which approaches at 90 degree angles to their built-in lines of communication. It has been proved that a highly dynamic group can force far greater disruption on a linear organization than their numbers or importance justify.

The typical organization chart shows a hierarchy of superordinates connected by neat lines to their subordinates. These lines are equivalent to the words "communicates with." Most lines run vertically. The typical linear organization is therefore only designed to permit a flow of communication in vertical channels. One is meant to talk with the person directly above and the person directly below one's position on the chart. One does not, theoretically, talk horizontally with people in different divisions or companies, because that would confuse the machinelike flow of communication. The flow runs in straight lines from worker to supervisor to manager to executive—and back the other way.

The introduction of staff functions confuses but does not change the basic picture. The staff works on a particular level of the organization and advises at this level so that the basic flow of orders is not significantly changed.

The effect of this linear patterning is to make the organization dependent on its ability to maintain the vertical flow of communication. Any input which interrupts the vertical flow places extreme stress on the organization. For instance, a man in a chain can become sick or have problems with his family which cause him to be distracted. These realities will affect his performance on the job. In most organizations he is the only person at his point in the chain who is "entitled" to maintain the vertical flow of communication. The successful operation of the internal chain will be endangered by external horizontal input which influences him.

The take-over bid is another example of how strong horizontal input can affect the internal dynamics of linear organizations. An attempt to take over a company consumes the time and psychic energy of countless employees. Indeed, if the attempt is successful, the company can be so thoroughly shaken from top to bottom that it ceases to operate with an acceptable degree of efficiency. So far businessmen have shown little understanding of the dangers in rapid and extensive changes in personnel following a change in top management. It is still assumed, amazingly often, that morale factors are not truly significant to profitability. Human beings are still seen as replaceable cogs.

An obvious example of the vulnerability of linear organizations to horizontal input is the ability of demonstrations, protests, and lawsuits to trigger disruptive turbulence in these organizations. In 1969, for instance, a very small group issued a demand that the National Council of Churches and its participating denominations pay "reparations" to black people. The demand threw the entire liberal Protestant establishment into chaos. The National Council of Churches became unable to make decisions. In addition, people in the denominations spent countless hours and huge sums of money attempting to discover what should be done with a simple demand for cash.

Linear organizations are vulnerable to horizontal input because they lack redundancy in their lines of communication. If one person is unable to make necessary decisions, the whole chain of command may be affected. If several people are unable to make decisions, the whole organization will be seriously imperiled.

LINEAR ORGANIZATIONS CAN ONLY MAKE LINEAR DECISIONS: THEY NECESSARILY EXTEND EXISTING PATTERNS. The first weakness of linear organizations discussed above is now generally understood. The second weakness to be examined here is not yet generally understood. It stems from the fact that the output channels of linear organizations operate linearly just as their input channels operate linearly. An organization which operates as a machine at the input end inevitably operates as a machine at the output end.

It is unrealistic to ask a bureaucracy to behave systemically. It is strictly bound by the nature of its output channels. It is unrealistic, for instance, to expect college bureaucrats to act in terms of the world view of young people. If they did not hold bureaucratic positions, there might be some hope these people would understand the world view of the young. But tied to their positions, they can only behave bureaucratically. They will be forced to behave in this way unless and until the organization shifts its mode from linear to systemic. The only type of change in output available to a linear organization is switching emphasis from one line to another. Voluntary organizations, for instance, may have a program emphasis running for one or two years; they then switch to a new program emphasis. It is possible to switch from one line of output to another, but it is impossible to change fundamentally the *kind* of output and still maintain a bureaucratic structure. Linear bureaucratic organizations can only take linear actions.

LINEAR ORGANIZATIONS CAN BE EASILY OVERLOADED AND UNDERLOADED. Overload and underload are increasingly common realities for many people. Overload can be described as a situation in which an individual or a group which is charged with making decisions gets flooded with more information and responsibilities than it can handle. Underload, on the other hand, is a situation in which an individual or a group responsible for making decisions does not have enough information to make intelligent decisions or enough possibilities for action to make it feel relevant.

Every president of a large institution, including the President of the United States, faces the fact that there will inevitably be more information and decisions needing his attention than he has time and energy to handle. In linear organizations, people down the chain know that decisions should be made at levels above them. Therefore, information and the responsibility for making decisions get passed up the chain until they reach the person who is charged with making decisions. The effect of this passing the buck up the chain is that people who are charged with making decisions get rapidly overloaded. President Truman's sign "The buck stops here" shows how clearly he understood this reality. People who actually make decisions have desks piled with paper and lines of people waiting at their door to get some decision or other. Because they are forced to handle too much information and to make too many decisions, the effectiveness of overloaded people tends to diminish.

It is not usually recognized that overload conditions

inherently distort information. The more information there is around, the greater the likelihood that decisions will be made on the basis of irrelevant or incomplete information. Overload makes it increasingly difficult to separate the wheat from the chaff. Recognizing this reality, some bureaucracies churn out mountains of information—in order to conceal the fact that most of it is chaff. Overload is today often deliberately used as a means of distorting information.

Because of the degree of overload, bottlenecks develop. Two kinds of responses to bottlenecks are possible. First, the organization continues to use linear functioning and operates less and less successfully until it eventually collapses. Alternatively, *unauthorized* decision-making nodes emerge where effective decisions *are* made. This practice too, however, will lead to the eventual collapse of the organization unless the various decision-making nodes learn how to communicate with each other rather than struggling on the basis of their relative power.

Many of the main support structures in today's society are chronically overloaded. Indeed there is now a danger of widespread collapse of overloaded structures. Three of these overloaded structures should be mentioned here. One is the judicial structure. It is widely known that in some areas of the United States, particularly in the Northeast, it can take years for a case to come to court. The judicial structure in America is so clogged by overload that it simply does not work.

The electrical production structure is also severely overloaded. Again, the most chronic area is the Northeast—New York City in particular—where inefficiency, lack of planning, very high levels of consumption coupled with the objections of conservationists have caused a crisis which apparently cannot be solved by those presently responsible for electrical production in the area. In the summer of 1970, two power stations in the New York area failed, requiring the overload of other systems to handle the breakdown. Other areas of the country can expect similar crises in the near future—crises whose effects will be greatly compounded because of an emerging shortage of all natural sources of energy: oil, coal, gas, etc.

A third major support structure which is chronically over-loaded is the communication structure: phones, wire serv-ices, the post office, and the airlines. This reality has been temporarily and partially disguised by the 1969–71 recession. The Northeast—which leads the country in extent of collapse—has already had massive communication failures. The communications structure has not been rethought in terms of present realities. It is not designed to carry present and future loads. There is still no sign that society has decided to begin the process of reconceiving communication methods in true system terms or that it has realized that communication will be more important than transportation in the future.

LINEAR ORGANIZATIONS ARE SUSCEPTIBLE TO THE PETER PRINCIPLE. Simply stated, the Peter Principle states that in a linear organization people tend to rise to a level of responsi-bility which they cannot handle. Every person tends to rise to his own level of incompetence. A book has been written to illustrate the principle, and the reader is referred to that book, *The Peter Principle*, for examples.

Given the points we have already made, the Peter Principle requires some restatement. It should actually read: every person tends to rise to his own level of marginal competence. Most frequently the principle works this way: people are generally not promoted to jobs they cannot do at all—rather, they get into jobs which they cannot do well. This is why a person who conforms to the Peter Principle infuriates those around him. If he were glaringly incompetent, he would be fired or demoted. Since he does part of his job adequately, his boss has difficulty stating why he should be fired.

Another factor which reinforces the effect of the Peter Principle is the hiring and promotion procedures of linear organizations. Let us take the average university as an exam-

ple. Most hiring of new faculty is done by a faculty committee composed of senior faculty with tenure. More often than
not these senior faculty have been resting on their laurels for
a long time. Consequently, their competence has diminished.
When they come to hire new faculty, they naturally tend to
avoid hiring men whose competence exceeds their own. As a
result, university faculty have become progressively less competent, because truly competent men are screened out. In
addition, even if a competent man gets hired, he will often
fail to be promoted because his ideas will seem heretical to
the senior faculty on the promotions committee. The same
pattern, of course, affects secondary and primary schools.

LINEAR ORGANIZATIONS ARE CAPABLE OF REPRODUCING
THEIR TYPE. This weakness of linear organizations can be
stated in a different way: bureaucracies can only think
bureaucratically. What happens, therefore, when a bureaucracy is confronted with a new situation about which it must
do something? For example, what behavior can we anticipate
when the federal government decides it wants to do something about poverty or education or the environmental
crisis?

A bureaucracy can take one of three actions. First, it can
ignore the new situation. Second, it can create a new set of
linear patterns and graft these onto an existing bureaucracy.
Third, it can create a separate bureaucracy to deal with the
new situation. None of these actions permits escape from the
basic reality that bureaucracies do not have the capacity to
create systemic organization patterns to cope with systemic
problems such as the environmental crisis or poverty. Let us
examine these three alternatives.

First, problems can be ignored. For several years, those
who best understood the potentials of computers warned
that the society's technological infrastructure was vastly
inadequate for present and future loads. In 1969, for instance,
the use of telephone lines by computers was running far
ahead of phone company expectations. It is virtually impos-

sible to get a telephone call in or out of the new CBS building in New York City between 10:00 and 2:00 on working
days. The same problem exists on Wall Street. The post
office has operated beyond capacity for years, and service, as
well as ·efficiency, has declined steadily. One of the most
serious dangers confronting America today is a total collapse
of the technological infrastructure. Indeed, the collapse is
already sufficiently extensive that we have recently been
forced to deal with some of the *symptoms* of this crisis. We
still, however, have not perceived the nature of the *overall*
crisis.

A similar lack of perception exists in other areas. For
example, since the early sixties, a few educators and socio-
economists have stated that young people and minority
groups must have power to make decisions about how to live
if they are not to opt out of the society or disrupt it. In particular, it was stressed that minority groups must decide
for themselves in which directions they wish to develop and
how resources are to be committed. Minority-group leaders
have repeated this statement on many occasions. Young
people have made the same statement: "Let me run my own
life." But the bureaucracies have ignored the demand for
the right to an independent life-style. They have also ignored
the problems to which these people pointed.

In addition bureaucracies, particularly the religious and
welfare bureaucracies, have almost totally ignored the question of ensuring human rights in a cybernetic era. They have
largely ignored the issue raised by the ability of machines
and computers to produce more than men, with higher
quality and lower cost. They have largely ignored the issue
of personal dignity in a time of electronic bugging and computer memories. They have largely ignored the issue of medical experimentation on social outcasts and the indigent.
While there is today growing recognition that ensuring the
dignity of man in the cybernetic era will require new steps,
we have left ourselves little time to imagine and implement
the necessary measures.

Let us now turn to examples of the second type of action: a bureaucracy can graft a response to a new situation onto an existing bureaucracy. This happened in 1968 within the National Council of Churches. The council decided there was a racial, economic, and social crisis in the nation. The "Crisis in the Nation" program was created. It was meant to be different in style and scope to those programs presently existing. However, it was grafted onto existing structures. As a result, almost as soon as the program came into existence, it lost its credibility because it assumed the vices of bureaucratic organization: incompetence in top management, lack of communication with the people the program was intended to serve, general inefficiency within the program itself, and commitments and promises broken.

The response of many corporations to the environment movement has been of a similar type: grafting a few slipshod policies and programs—just enough to make a reasonable-sounding press release—onto existing patterns. For instance, during the peak of the environment movement, several companies were moved to issue policy papers favoring clean air and water and to set up special committees to advise on pollution control. The fact that American industry could state so little of substance seemed at the time not to worry most people. Corporate managers appeared unconcerned and even seemed to want public gratitude for public-relations statements.

Similarly, those schools and universities which responded to the environment generally did so by grafting a little new material onto existing programs. Interested teachers simply added a new course to the catalog. Where new organizations were created, they were usually placed under existing tenure, curriculum, and administrative committees. A report to the President's Environmental Quality Council clearly stated that university programs in ecology could only succeed if they were free of existing bureaucratic control and allowed to develop their own style of organization. The report was essentially ignored. There was no true recognition that systemic organization and linear organization are not on the same conceptual plane.

There is a special case of this pattern of grafting one bureaucratic structure onto another which must be recognized. It is exceedingly common for one section of a bureaucracy to borrow successful programs or procedures from another section and to apply these programs to situations for which they were not designed. It is thought that by borrowing a successful program, one can repeat the success. But programs are successful because they are designed for a specific situation: they cannot be automatically transferred to a different situation.

In the last chapter we looked at an example of borrowing programs. The idea of using the government as employer of last resort is borrowed from the experience of the public-works projects during the thirties. However, the idea is now totally inappropriate because the situation today is entirely different.

The third possible response to a new situation is the creation of a separate bureaucracy to handle it. Indeed, this is the most common practice. For instance, a special bureaucracy was created to handle the federal poverty program. A special bureaucracy was created to advise the President on environmental policy. In New York City, a new citizen's committee forms during every crisis. The bureaucratic style is so habitual to Americans that if a group of three or more people agree on a subject they should study, they elect a president, a treasurer, and a secretary to promote the topic.

LINEAR ORGANIZATIONS TEND NOT TO PASS UNFAVORABLE INFORMATION UP OR DOWN THE CHAIN. Unfavorable information is not passed up the chain because the person passing it fears it may reflect on his competence and performance, and he is afraid of the reaction of his boss. Unfavorable information is not passed down the chain for the same reason.

A dramatic example of this process is that right up until

the shelling of Berlin, Hitler was told that German troops were winning in the East. Similarly, President Nixon was told that the spring 1970 invasion of Cambodia would not seriously affect the domestic scene. Suppression of information about the massacre in 1968 at My Lai, South Vietnam, extended into the top levels of the United States Army, Department of Defense, and other agencies of the federal government. Universities are accustomed to suppressing information about such things as faculty competence, student opinions on campus affairs, and pregnancies. The judicial system works on the principle that cases are won because certain information fails to enter the decision-making process. A litigant in an accident suit exaggerates the extent of the injury and his inability to recover his health. A defense attorney in a murder case attempts to build a pattern of information which suggests his client is innocent and moves to eliminate information which suggests his client is guilty. Within today's system, lawyers cannot be seekers after truth. They must attempt to manipulate the flow of information to favor their client.

People have only recently recognized the extent to which information in hospitals fails to move up and down care chains. This failure may result from carelessness, incompetence, or overload. For example, a nurse may fail to watch or accurately read a patient's vital indicators. As a result, the patient becomes sicker and may die. In the case of death, the patient's family is told that chances for recovery were slim in any case, and there was a sudden, uncontrollable turn for the worse. The real crisis in health care is not funding, facilities, and personnel. Rather it is a crisis of confidence in the ability, opportunity, and intention of nurses, doctors, and hospitals to give patients the care they require. The reality of this situation is dramatically shown in the number of malpractice suits. In the past, malpractice suits were a rarity: patients and their relatives trusted the doctor. Today, there is a growing belief that much health care is unsatisfactory.

Malpractice insurance is therefore a heavy, and growing, burden on all doctors.

FINALLY, LINEAR ORGANIZATIONS ARE ONLY CAPABLE OF CONTROLLING PEOPLE WHO WISH TO BE CONTROLLED. People who work in bureaucracies usually like to take orders. They do not really want to make decisions. It is for this reason that they move into bureaucratic organizations. This is not always true, of course: some people work in bureaucracies of necessity, but by far the larger number do so by choice. Bureaucracies tend to become staffed by people who do not want to make decisions. They are happy to go by the book and follow existing rules and regulations. In effect, they do not make decisions. They extend existing, linear trends.

Those people who do wish to make decisions to invent new programs and to develop new ideas tend to move out of bureaucratic organizations, or they simply stay away from them. Such people do not wish to become cogs in someone else's wheel. They are their own men. Increasingly, creative and talented people of all ages stay away from bureaucracies when they are able to do so.

One dramatic example of this tendency is the federal government. People are increasingly unwilling to accept major responsibilities in the federal bureaucracy. But the same process of selective outflow affects other major bureaucratic institutions. It affects corporations, many of which have come to perceive that their survival depends on intelligence and talent rather than on the traditional supports of money and power. It affects the Church, which attracts men with bureaucratic minds when it needs movers and healers. It affects the medical and legal professions, which are filled with people attracted by large incomes and high prestige.

One of the most serious aspects of the present situation is that young people are determined to move out of linear organizations even if this means they must work in jobs which seem meaningless to them. A recent *Wall Street Journal* story examined the dropout who, for example, drove a cab. In today's conditions, society cannot afford to lose those who are most capable of and most willing to make decisions. We must set up new institutional styles which will effectively permit those who are able to function nonbureaucratically to be involved in policy decisions.

Nonbureaucratic organizations of this type are already springing up. These nonbureaucratic organizations cannot be dominated by bureaucracies, for their complex systemic patternings are not effectively altered by attempts at linear control. In a sense, a move toward higher levels of organization is already taking place in our society. The primary pattern today is not the loss of past methods of control but rather the gain of new, effective ones. Linear organizations cannot deal with our present crises. Systemic organizations have the capacity to act effectively, and these are already beginning to develop.

To summarize, linear organizations have inherent and serious weaknesses. Their weaknesses prevent these organizations from making the kind of decisions which are necessary in a time of dynamic change. Because the world does *not* work like a machine, linear organizations are incapable of making appropriate judgments about the real world.

There is no suggestion in this chapter that those acting within bureaucracies are evil. Each bureaucracy—labor unions, lawyers, educators, churchmen, etc.—is locked into a structure. They are forced to act in ways which they often perceive as undesirable but they do not know how to escape. The remainder of this book tries to show that process and cooperation offer meaningful options to those who are now trapped.

In the following chapter we will explore the fundamental reasons for the failure of bureaucratic organizations. We will discover why the federal government, ecology groups, schools, churches, and corporations have failed to respond adequately to the environmental crisis. Chapter 5 will set out a scenario which shows readers who are still unconvinced of the impotence of bureaucracies the trends which can be expected to develop if we fail to develop systemically organized institutions.

4 *TYPES OF AUTHORITY,*
STRUCTURAL AND SAPIENTIAL

Up to this point, we have been primarily engaged in demonstrating that the industrial era is ending. We have argued that people in the abundance regions have already entered a new world and that we must now act effectively to create the institutions required to live in this new world. Our industrial-era patterns of action were successful so long as our powers were limited. They have now become dysfunctional. Today we must learn how to choose the directions in which we wish to go. Failure to make intelligent choices will lead to the destruction of the environment on which man's survival depends.

This line of argument challenges the generally accepted belief that tinkering with the present system will suffice to deal with future problem/possibilities. It is still rather generally argued that there is no need for any fundamental change in policies and that the patternings of the industrial era can continue indefinitely. The conventional wisdom is that the present bureaucratic mode of organization will suffice for the future. In effect, people believe that no matter how bad things become, we will muddle through.

The last chapter provided a description of the way in which linear bureaucratic organizations operate. We saw that in today's conditions they operate very badly, both in their own terms and in terms of their effect on the environment. This chapter will analyze the growing ineffectiveness of the linear mode of organization. We will discuss the present situation in terms of the diminishing acceptance of structural authority based on position and the need for an increasing acceptance of sapiential authority based on knowledge. The industrial era is based on structural authority. Since structural authority is no longer accepted or effective, we must find a different form of authority on which to base the operation of society.

The world view of the industrial era

In order to prove that we need fundamental change we must show that industrial-era patternings will not solve our problems or develop our possibilities. It is only if the world view of the industrial era is fundamentally inadequate for the future that we should adopt a different world view. If we can still use the institutional structures of the industrial era, it would be more realistic to accomplish needed reforms within the *existing* framework than through taking the time to invent new values and institutions.

What is the basic rationale of the industrial-era world view? It is that man must be ruled by structural authority. Certain people are seen as capable of holding power. The orders they hand down from the top of a pyramidal structure are *always* valid and must *always* be obeyed.

It was this assumption which made it possible to achieve such great feats during the nineteenth century. The railroads were built on the principle of structural authority. The assembly line is a perfect example of frozen structural authority. The principle of structural authority was also necessary to industrial-era warfare, which started under Napoleon but was carried to its peak of "perfection" in the First World War.

The individual within a structured authority system abandons his right to think for himself. In church and union, business and club, certain people hold structural authority and therefore have the right to wield power. The couplet

"Ours not to reason why,
Ours but to do or die"

perfectly expresses the mind-set of the industrial era.

The individual who fits within structural-authority systems was described by David Riesman, the American sociologist, as "other directed." An individual of this type makes no fundamental decisions for himself. His decision-making capacity atrophies for he follows the norms of the groups with which he associates.

Up to the present time, analyses of other-directedness have been in terms of its absolute value or lack of value to the individual. We, however, are concerned here with whether it fits *coming* conditions. We recognize that the industrial era could not have existed without this behavior pattern. The industrial era was made possible by the existence of other-directed individuals, obeying the dictates of those who held power.

It is clear, however, that the principle of structural authority is presently decaying. We must analyze whether the process of decay should be permitted to continue and, indeed, whether we have the capacity to control the process of decay.

A whole volume would not be adequate to examine fully the process by which structural authority is decaying. However, the process can be most dramatically traced in the operations of the military, where the commitment to structural authority was perhaps the greatest. Industrial-era military discipline was based on *immediate* and *total* obedience to orders. Penalties might eventually be levied against those responsible for military orders, but those who obeyed orders were not considered to be liable for legal trial and punishment.

The first break in this pattern probably occurred with the trial of Henry Wirz, who was accused of conspiracy to ill-treat and murder federal prisoners of war confined at the Andersonville prison camp during the American Civil War. Despite the evidence which showed that he was carrying out direct orders of a military superior, he was convicted and executed. The policy of holding soldiers responsible for obeying the orders of superiors was extended during the war between the British and the Boers at the beginning of the twentieth century.

Codification of this new pattern began to develop after the First World War. After the Second World War, large numbers of soldiers were tried for war crimes. In most cases, the statement that an action was taken on the direct order of a superior was considered no excuse, nor was it held to be an extenuating circumstance.

The advantage of being on the winning side became obvious. For example, if the United States and Britain had lost the Second World War, it seems clear that much of the bombing over Germany—notably that of Dresden—would have been considered a war crime. Given the fact of victory, those who participated in thousand-bomber raids on Germany were seen as heroes. If the Japanese had won the war after America dropped the atomic bomb, they would certainly have considered the Hiroshima and Nagasaki bombings war crimes.

The corrosive effect of the doctrine of war crimes on military discipline has become obvious in Vietnam. Many of the soldiers in Vietnam are unwilling to be there, for they were drafted to fight in a war they oppose. They therefore expect orders to be explained and justified. Their ability to act in this way is supported by the fact that they have the legal right—indeed, the legal obligation—to refuse to carry out any order which they believe would make them guilty of a war crime.

This situation is impossible from the point of view of effective industrial-era military discipline. Military effectiveness depends on orders being promptly obeyed. Military organization will eventually be paralyzed by a requirement that soldiers should have the right to challenge decisions on the basis of their own judgment of right or wrong.

The situation which is developing as a result of the war-crimes doctrine is intolerable for those who must command. But the situation is scarcely more tenable from the point of view of the individual soldier. He is now expected to be wise enough to know if the order he is being given is unlawful *before the fact*. Given the reality that the military will not be sympathetic to a soldier even if his case is, in fact, strongly based, a refusal to obey orders may result in a trial for mutiny.

For example, what would be the position of an American soldier who refused to enter Cambodia on the grounds that an invasion of a "neutral" country is illegal or to take part in the killing of "civilians" on the grounds that it was against the rules of war? Unless other systems of communication and control besides those of the military are operative, the case will often be dealt with in categories that the military can understand. Military categories still do not normally recognize the right of an individual soldier to make up his mind about whether to obey the command of an officer.

In these circumstances, it is not surprising that most soldiers still obey orders. However, for those who do, another trap is lurking. If they are profoundly unlucky, they may be among those who are caught up in a well-publicized case, such as My Lai, where war crimes were committed. In this case, the soldier may be condemned for his actions. Such a condemnation is evidence of scapegoat policies because only the naïve can believe that there have been only one or two massacres in Vietnam. Atrocities are part of the total picture in every war. Why then should a few individuals be singled out for punishment?

It is possible to trace a similar process of decay of structural authority in all other areas of the society: law, education, politics, etc. Today, the holding of a position does not guarantee that the individual can enforce orders given to his subordinates in the hierarchy.

The obsolescence of structural authority

At first sight, it is natural to assume that we are suffering from a decay in all authority and the capacity to take any decisions. Since every society must be based on some form of authority, the decay of present styles of authority will inevitably be seen as dangerous. For example, many of those who perceive a decline in authority today call for a return to earlier norms. In addition, they show a willingness to use power—law and order—to enforce these norms if it seems necessary.

We are not, however, experiencing the end of authority. It is not being argued that a soldier is entitled to disobey any order which displeases him. Rather, a soldier is expected to disobey certain orders which are defined as unlawful. A soldier is now told that he should refuse to obey an order, *when on the basis of his own judgment,* he believes it to be unlawful. He must, therefore, have sufficient knowledge to judge the lawfulness of an order. The new form of authority depends on the competence and knowledge of each individual. It is therefore convenient to call it sapiential authority.

Those who claim that we are suffering from a decay in authority miss the point. We are actually confronted with a struggle between two fundamentally opposing viewpoints about the proper way to organize a society. Since the opposition between these viewpoints is so fundamental, efforts to reimpose order by strengthening structural authority can only lead to negative reactions on the part of those who support sapiential-authority principles. Many of those who oppose structural authority do so on the grounds that it violates human dignity and will lead to the destruction of the human race. They are therefore unwilling to acquiesce in its perpetuation.

We cannot yet usefully discuss whether it is reasonable and fair to give the individual the right and responsibility to employ sapiential authority. We shall return to this issue, but we must first discover how far this new sapiential-authority principle has come to govern the actual operation of the society without ever having been clearly identified. For while the recognized organizing principle of the society remains structural authority, ever larger parts of the culture actually operate on the basis of sapiential authority.

The principles enunciated at the Nuremburg trials were, of course, an early and direct attack on the principle of structural authority even if they were not perceived in this way by many. Since the Nuremburg trials—but without our recognizing the fact—patterns of structural authority have been heavily undermined in institution after institution, and claims for the validity of sapiential authority have been widely advanced. The examples which follow are chosen at random to give a range of areas in which people are demanding the right to make decisions for themselves. (The reader should be able to imagine at least as many other areas for himself.)

■ The industrial-era organizing principle of schools and universities is that the professor is there to "teach" and the student is there to "learn." Educational establishments are organized around the belief that the very fact of being a teacher or professor guarantees competence. Competence is proved by a person's title rather than his performance. Today, however, students are increasingly making up their minds about the value of their teachers in terms of an ability to teach "relevantly." Students are claiming that they have the sapiential authority to perceive when a teacher is competent and when he is not. They are denying that competence and authority are guaranteed by the possession of a title.

■ The astronauts have been involved in several brief, but hot, arguments with mission control, whose very title denotes structural authority. The astronauts have claimed that their nearness to the situation invests them with greater authority than mission control. This is obviously a claim to sapiential authority.

■ The infallibility of the Pope is being challenged. It is no longer accepted by large parts of the Catholic Church that the Pope is necessarily correct even when he speaks ex cathedra. The doctrine of papal infallibility, conceived in the industrial era, is dying with it. Indeed, right from the beginning, Popes have avoided using their powers under this doctrine, because they know that its use would precipitate schism in the Church. Those who dissent from the doctrine of papal infallibility are claiming that they possess the sapiential authority to make judgments. They are denying that the position as head of the hierarchy of the Catholic Church conveys an inherent right to make unchallengable decisions.

■ The right of the President of the United States to make decisions based on his structural authority is also increasingly being challenged. It is argued that if the President has a sufficiently good case, he should be able to convince the country by the use of sapiential authority. While certain exceptions to this new view are still recognized—such as imminent national danger—the intensity of the attempt to limit the use of Presidential structural authority grows rapidly.

The converse of this view is also being advanced. It was commonly argued in the past that the very fact of being President gave the right to take decisions because the President had data not available to the public. This approach is now being challenged on the grounds that it is not the classified details which are important in making major decisions but rather the sweep of events which can be known by all. Indeed, some people now perceive that the structural authority available to the President necessarily biases his data. The President, therefore, actually often has less usable information than that available to others.

■ Until recently, the media were arbiters of the thinking of a large part of the American people. They had achieved the equivalent of structural authority over much of the country, particularly the East. People felt that they should share the views of certain editorialists and columnists. This feeling was part of the pattern of other-directedness.

Recently, a growing number of people, including Vice-President Agnew, have been arguing that the media should not have structural authority. In this area, also, the citizen is learning that he should think for himself rather than take the conclusions pressed upon him by others.

■ There has been a steady rise in the number of people who declare themselves independents rather than recognize the structural authority of any particular political party. Such individuals are claiming the right to determine for themselves the stands they should take on various issues.

■ The various liberation movements—black, Indian, Mexican, women, youth, homosexual—are all making the same argument. They are stating that they are no longer willing to accept structural authority as the source of their values. They say that they themselves are the best judges of the ways in which they should live. The life-styles they value are very different from those presently dominating the society, and they believe they are entitled to choose the life-styles which please them.

During the industrial era, societies moved toward homogeneity. The ideal was that people should be cogs—mutually replaceable cogs—in the machine society. The need was to eliminate those differences in workers which would make them less than perfect replacements for each other.

This approach was essential if bureaucracies were to be effective. The ideal of bureaucratic organization is that the replacement of one person by another in the chain of command makes no difference to the way the bureaucracy works. Now that we know that this ideal is impossible, we should expect that those groups which have previously felt most constrained by bureaucratic stereotyping will be most unwilling to continue to conform to it.

We have cited only a few of the areas in which sapiential authority is replacing structural authority: limitations of space prevent continuation. If one is searching for a single key to the present process of change in the United States and the world, this shift in forms of authority is probably the most relevant.

Is sapiential authority possible?

Is this movement away from structural authority and toward sapiential authority realistic or should we attempt to reverse it? We could, of course, dodge the question by arguing that the movement away from structural authority is so powerful that there is no way in which reversal can occur, even if it would be desirable. But such an approach is fundamentally unsatisfactory. Our most urgent need is to discover whether the movement toward sapiential authority is increasing the chances of man's survival or diminishing them.

The movement toward sapiential authority is essential. This statement is based on system theory which has developed in recent years and which enables us to understand the conditions under which a system can survive. (A system in this discussion is any group of interlinked phenomena which it is convenient to examine together.) Systems are always changing, and the patterns and criteria needed to communicate within them are therefore also always changing. Human systems survive and develop when there are decision makers to reverse divergences from desired norms and when these decision makers receive the information they need in order to make effective decisions.

Structural authority systems are set up to meet the first of these conditions. Certain people are made responsible for the decision-making process. It is assumed that they will act in a way which will deal effectively with identified problems.

However, structural-authority systems necessarily fail to meet the second of these conditions. Indeed, they ensure the distortion of information flowing in the structure. Nobody brings bad news to his boss if he can avoid it, for one of the most fundamental of human patterns is the rejection of people who bring bad news.

There are, of course, some people who refuse to fall into this trap. They insist that their subordinates tell them the truth as they see it. In this situation, however, the system ceases to be based on structural authority: it moves into a sapiential-authority pattern. The individual with power chooses to make decisions on the basis of the most accurate information he can obtain rather than reach his own arbitrary conclusions.

People who wish to make decisions that are related to the real world must use sapiential-authority patterns. Sapiential-authority patterns increase man's chances of survival, because they connect him more effectively to the real world.

The need to recognize sapiential authority

Structural authority is infeasible in the cybernetic era we are entering. We are therefore being forced to recognize the shift from structural authority to sapiential authority. This does not mean that we can expect an immediate and total replacement of structural authority by sapiential authority. It does mean, however, that all future decisions must be evaluated in terms of whether they move us toward or away from sapiential-authority patterns. Likewise, policies which are based on structural authority must be highly suspect.

There are still many who argue that this change in the society is impossible. Such a conclusion condemns man to his own self-destruction.

There is no doubt that the odds against man's survival are now very high. However, there is no reason to believe that the odds are insuperable. The time has come when we must discover the precise nature of the challenge which confronts us and act to overcome it. We should rapidly move past the point where we agonize about the desperate nature of our predicament. Agonizing wastes time that can be used in the invention of new ways to solve our problems. Diagnosis has a fascination which often prevents action.

We need to perceive the directions in which we are presently moving. We need to know the directions in which we wish to move. We need to create methods which will make it possible for mankind to evolve a world view in which more of the potentials of the earth and the human race can be achieved.

However, before we can discover answers to these problems/possibilities, we must understand the degree to which our present condition is similar to that of past eras and the degree to which it is unique. We must know the extent to which we can learn from history and the areas, if any, in which we must invent new responses.

Any significant change in the conditions in which a group lives acts to decrease the relevance of existing wisdom and existing ways of doing things. Decisions based on past experience will often be profoundly counterproductive if they are applied after conditions have changed.

Sapiential authority is therefore essential in dynamic conditions. In dynamic conditions those most competent to understand the emerging realities should have the opportunity to evaluate them and to determine the appropriate pattern of decision making.

Arnold Toynbee, the British historian, has linked the rise and fall of cultures to their success or failure in permitting sapiential authority to be used to deal with emerging realities. When a culture becomes too rigid to handle successfully the new conditions which confront it, it collapses, and another culture arises to take its place. The life cycle of a culture depends on two things: first, the speed at which fundamentally new realities arise, and second, the ability of the culture to bring people who have sapiential authority about the new realities into the decision-making process.

One of the aspects of a well-functioning society is that structural authority and sapiential authority coincide. Crises will occur however a society is organized, and they may leave no time to perceive and judge new patterns of sapiential authority. The survival of societies in conditions of rapid change depends, therefore, on the degree to which those who have achieved sapiential authority *about the new conditions* are placed in positions which attest their right to make decisions. Structural authority saves time in emergencies, but it can only be useful if it is actually backed by sapiential authority. One of the reasons for the relatively long-run success of Britain, in historical terms, was the very high degree of mobility in the British culture. Britons have always accepted structural authority. The relative permanence of the system was based on the fact that those who gained sapiential authority were moved into structural-authority positions, and those who failed to keep up with the times lost their positions of structural authority. For a long period Britain had, in effect, a sapiential-authority system disguised in a structural-authority uniform. The failure of Britain in the postwar years has coincided with the breakdown of this pattern.

The seriousness of the crisis which now confronts us can be perceived once we understand that no culture has so far been able to deal with the massive shifts inherent in changes of era. The shift between the hunting and gathering era and the agricultural era involved the collapse of some groups and the rise of others. The shift between the agricultural era and the industrial era led to the decline of some nations and the rise of others. If we should follow past patterns, we can anticipate that the shift between the industrial era and the cybernetic era will cause further changes in dominant cultures. Specifically, we can anticipate that the West will lose its present dominant position.

The long sweep of history may well show that the West could not move effectively into the cybernetic era. If historians are alive to look back from the twenty-second century, they will probably see a profound alteration in influence patterns during the last third of the twentieth century. But, unfortunately, there will only be a long sweep to human history if the West chooses to give up her position of dominance freely. The West cannot be overcome by nations having greater power. The use of the presently available destructive power would eliminate mankind.

In this regard our present situation is ahistorical. Many

cultures have collapsed: there are more dead cultures than live ones. In all past cases, cultures have either decayed from within, or they have been overwhelmed from without. New and vibrant cultures have taken the place of dying ones. Today, however, the survival of the world requires that the presently dominant cultures of the world change their own means of operation fundamentally—*without outside coercion and without internal collapse.*

Such a task has never been accomplished. This task is made even more difficult because the required pace of change is far greater than ever before.

We could succeed, however, because we have two advantages which have not existed at any previous time. First, we have the advantage of free time. Second, we have the advantage of an effective communications infrastructure.

The potential of free time

In every past culture, the toil of almost all the population was required to permit the survival of the population. The level of action required to manage change between eras could not be achieved because people lacked the time to think through what needed to be done.

Today a very large amount of free time is available. Unfortunately, it is still being very largely used for the ingurgitation and regurgitation of information conceived within the obsolete world view of the industrial era. So long as this situation continues, our free time will not help us. Indeed, most present uses of our free time keep us away from any real possibility of dealing with our problems.

The existence of free time does, however, provide enormous potential if we should resolve to use it to discover the nature of the real world in which we are living and the steps which could be taken to manage the transition into the cybernetic era. There is already clear evidence that many, particularly among the young, have a basic understanding of our new era. They could engage successfully in the process of clarifying their vision if they were encouraged to do so. Instead, most of them are continuously informed that their attempt to perceive new possibilities is idealistic and irrelevant to real problems.

As we think about our attitudes to the young, we should be aware that failure to take advantage of the potential of their free time is already turning it into a threat. The level of the threat will continue to rise so long as we do not provide an outlet for available energies. People who desire to help create a new world and who are deprived of an opportunity to do so will necessarily become frustrated. Frustrated people are likely to turn to violence or to cop out into a life centered around drugs and meaningless sex.

The potential of the communications infrastructure

In previous periods, there was no way for ideas to be rapidly communicated, even if they were successfully generated. The methods of passing ideas from one person to another were so limited and the environment was so constraining that even when some people were fully aware of a coming crisis, they were unable to do anything significant to prevent it. The population could not be informed of the nature of the choices open to them.

Today the mass media are capable of moving new ideas effectively as soon as they are conceived. As in the case of our use of free time and our educational practices, however, we are prevented from acting imaginatively by the world view we hold. The media are used almost entirely for amusement and not for the movement of information. Those media which do perceive a responsibility for moving information do so in such a pedantic way that they lose their audiences. Indeed, today very few schools or universities are using the media imaginatively as a means to develop new thinking.

We now have the ability to ensure that new ideas are made rapidly and widely available. But we cannot benefit from our ability until there has been a fundamental change in our patterns of thinking and acting. In the absence of a new mind-set, the media too will remain part of the overload problem instead of part of the educational solution.

Some thirty-five years ago, John Maynard Keynes, the great British economist, stated that "in the long run, it is ideas and not men that rule the world." As our present ideas are now incompatible with the survival of the world, it is the responsibility of all of us to create the new ideas we require and to move them into circulation as rapidly as possible.

The need for a new world view

The basic argument of this book is that the precondition for a solution to the ecological crisis is a fundamental change in the world view which determines our decisions. Most of the remainder of this book will try to help the reader perceive the world view which is necessary. However, before going on to this constructive aspect of the book, it is essential that the reader be fully aware why it is impossible to continue using the present world view.

The next chapter is not designed to be read as a whole unless the reader remains unconvinced that we face *certain* disaster if we continue along the present course. It is only if he still feels that tinkering with the industrial-era system can be effective that he is advised to work through the next chapter. He should recognize that each of the statistics and trends in the next chapter stand for a class of trends which appear every day in the newspaper. Indeed, it would be a useful discipline for the reader who is still convinced of the viability of present trends to read through his newspaper and magazines for a month or so, giving special attention to the development of present trends. The recent book, *Future Shock*, by Alvin Toffler will also be useful for this purpose. The work of Jay Forrester at the Massachusetts Institute of Technology, done under the auspices of the Club of Rome, is also useful for this purpose.

The next chapter can also be usefully examined as a checklist of various areas in which breakdown is to be expected. Such a checklist can have importance for the individual who is committed to trying to create a new world view, for it keeps him aware of the crises which he is likely to encounter as he tries to bring about change.

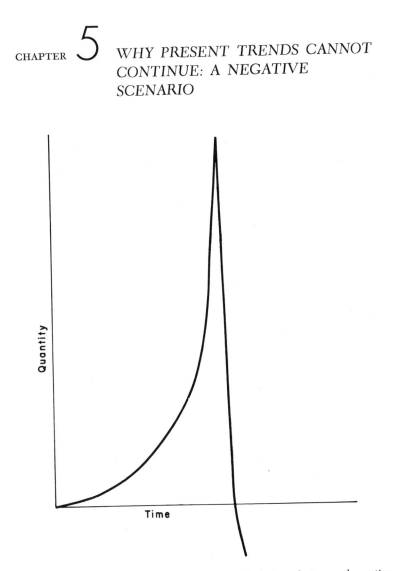

In today's world all curves are exponential. It is only in mathematics that exponential curves grow to infinity. In real life they either saturate gently or they break down catastrophically. It is our duty as thinking men to strive toward a gentle saturation.—Dennis Gabor

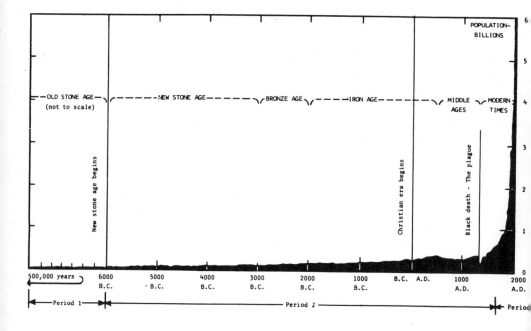

GROWTH OF HUMAN NUMBERS

It has taken all the hundreds of thousands of years of man's existence on earth for his numbers to reach three billion. But in only 40 more years population will grow to six billion, if current growth rates remain unchanged. If the Old Stone Age were in scale, its base line would extend 35 feet to the left!

Population Reference Bureau February 1962

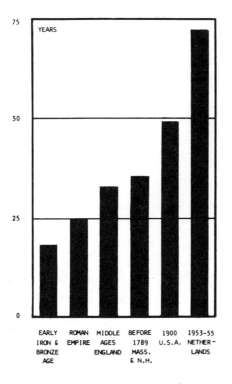

LIFE EXPECTANCY OVER THE AGES

Life expectancy at birth is believed to have been about 18 years in prehistoric times. It has quadrupled today in some of the Western industrialized countries. (Source: LENGTH OF LIFE: A STUDY OF THE LIFE TABLE by Louis I. Dublin, Alfred J. Lotka and Mortimer Spiegelman.)

Population Reference Bureau February 1962

"Assuming hopefully for the moment that no dictator, self-righteous planning board or omnipotent black box is going to make genetic selections for the coming generation, then who or what is? Not parents, certainly: they'll take the problem to their friendly neighborhood Certified Gene Architect." William Tenn in Alvin Toffler's FUTURE SHOCK

(1)

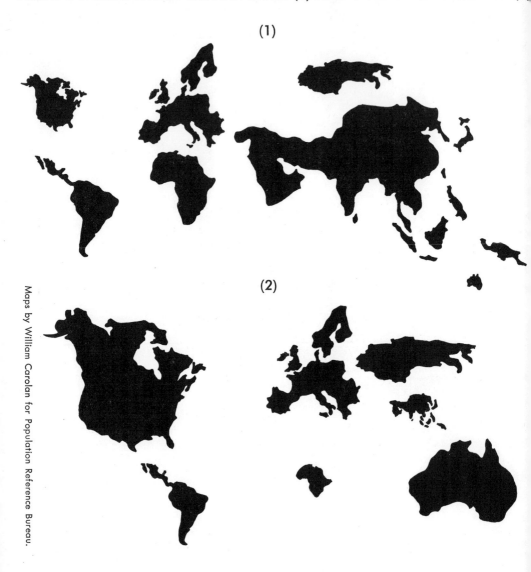

Maps by William Carolan for Population Reference Bureau.

(2)

"ANNUAL WORLD POPULATION GROWTH REACHES RECORD HIGH."

A map of the continents, scaled to population, is shown above (1). A stunning reversal of its size relationships is produced when the continents are weighted for per-capita Gross National Product (2). Asia, Africa and Latin America shrink dramatically. These three regions have nearly three-quarters of the world's population but they share only a quarter of its yearly income. The population and per capita GNP figures are: Africa—344 million people, $140; Asia—2,056 million people, $184; Europe—462 million people, $1,230; Latin America—283 million people, $385; North America—228 million people, $3,399; Oceania (including Australia and New Zealand)—19 million people, $1,857; and the Soviet Union—243 million people, $970. Sources: U.N. Population data for 1970, GNP figures from World Bank for latest available year.

Population Reference Bureau Press Release.

WATER REQUIRED FOR DAILY PER CAPITA FOOD PRODUCTION,
UNITED STATES AND INDIA

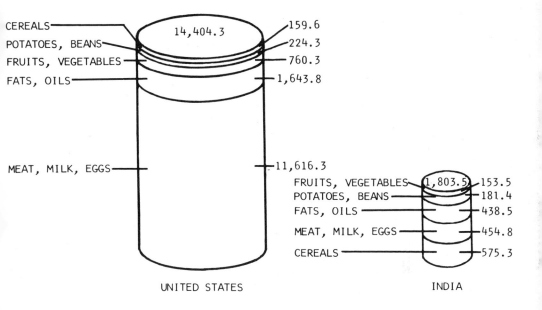

CEREALS — 14,404.3 — 159.6
POTATOES, BEANS — 224.3
FRUITS, VEGETABLES — 760.3
FATS, OILS — 1,643.8

MEAT, MILK, EGGS — 11,616.3

FRUITS, VEGETABLES — 1,803.5 — 153.5
POTATOES, BEANS — 181.4
FATS, OILS — 438.5
MEAT, MILK, EGGS — 454.8
CEREALS — 575.3

UNITED STATES   INDIA

Producing the daily food for one person requires eight times as much water in the United States as in India.
(Figures indicate liters. One gallon equals 3.785 liters.)

Source: Georg Borgstrom. TOO MANY: A STUDY OF THE EARTH'S BIOLOGICAL LIMITATIONS.

Population Reference Bureau June 1970

Some of the greatest disruptions of natural water patterns have been
caused by irrigation projects and the dams on which they depend. The
Kuriba Dam was built on the Zambesi River between Zambia and
Rhodesia. It displaced 29,000 farmers. After one bumper crop on the
new irrigated land there has been a succession of disasters: changes
in the water table, a need to plow in the rainy season, weed growth
in the lake, limiting the annual fish catch to 2,100 tons as compared
to the predicted 20,000 tons.

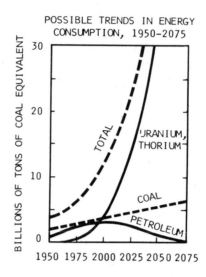

POSSIBLE TRENDS IN ENERGY CONSUMPTION, 1950-2075

Population Reference Bureau June 1970

The world's use of petroleum will peak around the turn of the century, while coal consumption continues to rise slowly. After about 1975, most of the increase in energy use will be provided by nuclear fuels.

Source: Harrison Brown, James Bonner, and John Weir. THE NEXT HUNDRED YEARS.

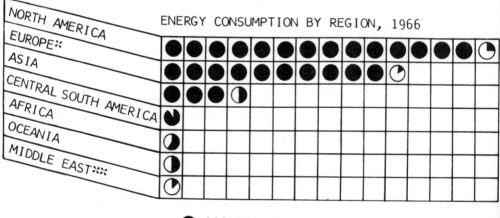

ENERGY CONSUMPTION BY REGION, 1966

⬤ 100,000 KILOWATT HOURS

* excludes U.S.S.R. U.S.S.R. total - 516,480 MKW

** includes Southern Yemen. Yemen figures not available. Cyprus (381MKW) is included with Europe.

Energy consumption, a good gauge of both pollution and development, is more than an order of magnitude greater in the West than other regions. Closing this gap while the West's energy use continues to rise would vastly increase the threats to the global environment.

Source: U.S. Federal Power Commission. WORLD POWER DATA, 1966.

Population Reference Bureau June 1970

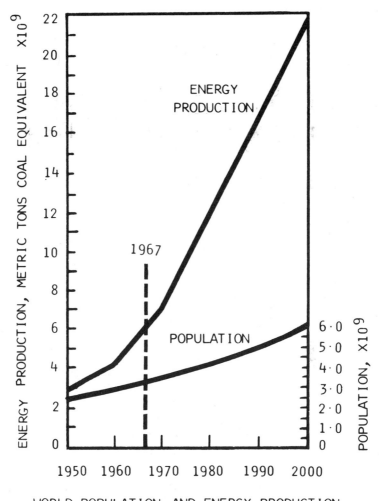

WORLD POPULATION AND ENERGY PRODUCTION

JOHN MC HALE WORLD ENERGY RESOURCES IN THE FUTURE
SEPTEMBER 1968

U.S. SHARE OF WORLD CONSUMPTION AND PRODUCTION, SELECTED MINERALS, 1967

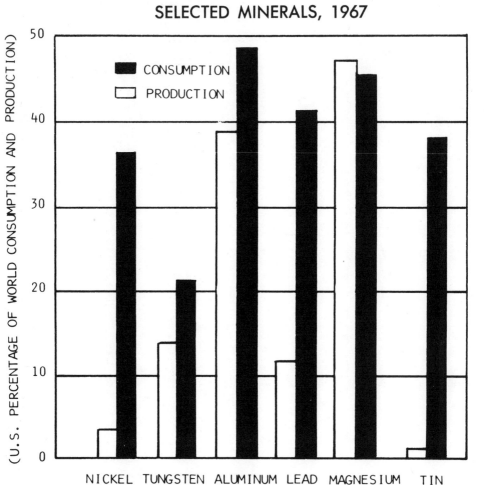

The wealthier a population, the more it taxes the world's natural resources. As U.S. real per capita income rises, so does the nation's dependency on mineral imports from abroad.

Source: STATISTICAL ABSTRACT OF THE UNITED STATES 1969. U.S. Department of Commerce.

Population Reference Bureau February 1970

The U.S. Bureau of Mines has formulated an interesting projection of our own nation's needs for the basic raw materials of industry in the year 2000. With respect to the leading metals, the projected increases in annual short tons of demand are as follows:

- [ ] Aluminum: from 4.4 million to nearly 35 million
- [ ] Copper: from 2 million to 6.5 million
- [ ] Iron: from 114 million to 171 million*
- [ ] Lead: from 1.3 million to 1.8 million.

For our supplies of these metals we are already drawing heavily on the rest of the world. But if 30 years hence the world at large were to claim as many pounds of metal per inhabitant as we do today, would the greatly increased amounts be readily forthcoming? At that time, we can anticipate that the human race will demand:

- [ ] 110 million short tons of aluminum, or over 13 times 1967 world production;
- [ ] 50 million short tons of copper, or nearly 9 times 1967 world production;
- [ ] 2,850 million short tons of iron, or over 7 times 1967 world production*;
- [ ] 33 million tons of lead, or nearly 11 times 1967 production.

---

* Pig iron including ferroalloys.   Population Reference Bureau June 1970

PERCENTAGE OF WORLD FOOD IMPORTS GOING TO WESTERN EUROPE, 1963-1965

Foodstuffs	Western Europe's Share of World Imports (%)
Frozen eggs	97.5
Oilseed cakes, meal	93.0
Bacon, ham	92.8
Fish oils	80.6
Oats	78.6
Poultry meat	78.0
Cheese, curd	77.3
Butter	77.0
Fish meal	72.7
Peanuts	71.6
Corn (maize)	68.8
Eggs	68.6
Meat	66.5
Wool	64.5
Barley	61.8
Copra	56.4
Meat extract	56.2
Sunflower seeds	54.6
Egg powder	54.5
Soybeans	53.5
Bran	52.8
Peas, beans	51.6
Meat meal	44.4
Non-fat milk solids	44.0
Cottonseed	37.7
Sugar	28.6
Wheat	22.3

Source: Georg Borgstrom. TOO MANY. New York: Macmillan Co., 1969. p. 239.

Population Reference Bureau June 1970

PERCENTAGE OF WORLD FOOD IMPORTS GOING TO THE UNITED STATES, 1963-1965

Foodstuffs	U.S. Share of World Imports (%)
Shrimp	71.9
Coffee	46.5
Tuna	45.4
Bananas	34.7
Cocoa	27.7
Fish (raw)	26.8
Beef	23.8
Canned Meat	23.5
Sugar	20.5

Source: Georg Borgstrom. TOO MANY. New York: Macmillan Co., 1969. p. 240.

Population Reference Bureau June 1970

DEVELOPMENT OF WORLD POPULATION

PERIOD	INCREASE FROM	DOUBLING IN YEARS	PERIOD	INCREASE FROM	DOUBLING IN YEARS
4500 B.C.—2500 B.C.	20 mill. to 40 mill.	2000	900—1700	320 mill. to 600 mill.	800
2500 B.C.—1000 B.C.	40 mill. to 80 mill.	1500	1700—1850	600 mill. to 1200 mill.	150
1000 B.C.—Birth of Christ	80 mill. to 160 mill.	1000	1850—1950	1200 mill. to 2500 mill.	100
Birth of Christ—A.D. 900	160 mill. to 320 mill.	900	1960—2000	3000 mill. to 6500 mill.	

United States National Commission for UNESCO—Special issue on 13th Annual Conference.

Population expert Heinz von Foerster calculates Doomsday as Friday, the 13th of November, 2026. That, according to his calculations, is when world population will begin doubling every 15 years.

An extremely conservative projection yields the following picture of world population density.

YEAR	POPULATION IN BILLIONS	PERSONS PER SQUARE MILE
1975	3.88	74.0
2025	9.08	178.3
2050	13.89	265.0
2400	5,330.39	101,677.2

In 1960, Manhattan island had a density of 77,194 persons per square mile.

"WHAT IS MAN THAT THOU ART MINDFUL OF HIM?"

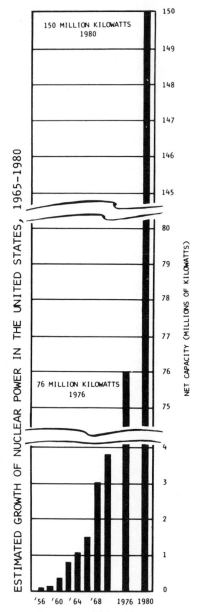

ESTIMATED GROWTH OF NUCLEAR POWER IN THE UNITED STATES, 1965–1980

NET CAPACITY (MILLIONS OF KILOWATTS)

150 MILLION KILOWATTS
1980

76 MILLION KILOWATTS
1976

'56 '60 '64 '68   1976 1980

Sources: John McHale, THE FUTURE OF THE FU-
TURE. New York: George Braziller, 1969. Projec-
tions for 1976 and 1980 given by Glenn T. Sea-
borg. Remarks at Financial Forum on Nuclear
Energy, Waldorf Astoria Hotel, New York City,
October 30, 1968.

Population Reference Bureau June 1970

Power plants take in cool water and return it heated: this is particularly important for atomic power plants. It has been estimated that if present exponential rates of power use continue, the temperature of waters and streams in the United States would rise 20° in the next 30 years.

TABLE I.—PROJECTIONS OF TOTAL FUEL USE

[Trillion B.t.u.'s]

	Bureau of Mines [1]	Ebasco [2]	Texas Eastern Transmission [3]	Sartorius & Co. [4]	AEC [5]
Coal:					
1965	12,313	12,300	11,705	12,222	([6])
1980	17,180–19,540	17,700	19,880	16,084	([6])
Yearly percent increase	2.2 – 3.1	2.5	3.6	1.8	-------------
Oil:					
1965	23,270	21,600	23,706	21,087	([6])
1980	35,981	32,200	40,174	29,943	([6])
Yearly percent increase	2.9	2.7	3.6	2.4	-------------
Natural gas:					
1965	16,603	18,000	16,241	16,301	([6])
1980	25,457	32,000	31,894	33,115	([6])
Yearly percent increase	2.9	3.9	4.6	4.8	-------------
Nuclear:					
1965	36	100	38	44	36
1980	4,075–6,435	9,200	4,757	13,330	8,703
Yearly percent increase	37.1 – 41.3	35.2	38.0	46.4	44.2
Waterpower:					
1965	1,901	2,000	660	660	1,901
1980	3,028	2,900	1,120	1,104	3,060
Yearly percent increase	3.2	2.5	3.6	3.5	3.2
Total:					
1965	54,124	54,000	52,350	50,314	([6])
1980	88,080	94,000	97,825	93,576	([6])
Yearly percent increase	3.3	3.7	4.2	4.2	-------------

[1] William A. Vogely and Warren E. Morrison (of the U.S. Bureau of Mines), "Patterns of U.S. Energy Consumption to 1980," IEEE Spectrum, September 1967, pp. 81 ff.
[2] "1967 Business and Economic Charts," Ebasco Services, Inc., New York, N.Y.
[3] "Competition and Growth in American Energy Markets, 1947–85," Texas Eastern Transmission Corp.
[4] Michael C. Cook, "Energy in the United States, 1960–85," published by Sartorius & Co. (member of the New York Stock Exchange).
[5] Based on a chart in the AEC's 1967 report to Congress.
[6] Not available.

Hearings, House of Representatives

Subcommittee of Committee on Government Operation September 5, 1968

Old Pennsylvania coal towns are collapsing into empty mines. City blocks are shifting and settling into collapsing tunnels and shafts around Scranton, Wilkes-Barre, and other Pennsylvania towns. 2,000,000 acres have already sunk and another 1,000,000 acres are expected to sink in the next 30 years. 200 urban centers in 28 states are threatened with sinking ground. Examples are: Birmingham, Springfield, Des Moines, Kansas City, Lexington, Detroit, Grand Rapids, St. Louis, Butte, Cleveland, Tulsa, Bellingham (Washington), and Fairmont (West Virginia). Long Beach (California) is sinking into empty oil pools and Manhattan's Battery area is sinking under the weight of buildings.

The tailings and slag from mines in the next 30 years will reach 19 billion tons: enough to cover 1,800,000 acres, or Delaware and Rhode Island combined. Presently 92,000 surface acres a year are undermined with no planning for surface development.

Estimated number of thermal generating plant sites 500-megawatt capacity and above for year 1990 [1]

NPS Region	Fossil-fuel plants by megawatt capacities					Nuclear plants by megawatt capacities				
	500 to 1,000	1,000 to 2,000	2,000 to 4,000	Over 4,000	Total	500 to 1,000	1,000 to 2,000	2,000 to 4,000	Over 4,000	Total
Northeast:										
Total sites	22	15	4	...	41	7	19	17	2	45
New sites	...	1	4	...	5	6	18	14	...	38
Cooling towers	3	5	...	...	8	2	4	3	...	9
Southeast:										
Total sites	15	12	7	...	34	10	22	21	7	60
New sites	3	3	...	...	6	8	18	14	5	45
Cooling towers	...	1	3	...	4	7	14	7	4	32
East Central:										
Total sites	30	26	5	1	62	1	10	8	2	21
New sites	5	9	1	1	16	...	8	7	2	17
Cooling towers	7	8	1	1	17	...	4	1	1	6
South Central:										
Total sites	37	31	23	1	92	3	9	9	1	22
New sites	17	12	19	1	49	3	9	9	1	22
Cooling towers	17	7	3	...	27	1	2	1	1	5
West Central:										
Total sites	11	12	2	...	25	3	6	9	1	19
New sites	1	5	...	...	6	2	4	5	...	11
Cooling towers	1	4	1	...	6	1	4	3	...	8
West:										
Total sites	14	19	4	1	38	4	7	9	13	33
New sites	4	4	1	...	9	4	6	9	12	31
Cooling towers	10	10	1	...	21	4	5	4	2	15
Total U.S.:										
Total sites	129	115	45	3	292	28	73	73	26	200
New sites	30	34	25	2	91	23	63	58	20	164
Cooling towers	38	35	9	1	83	15	33	19	8	75

[1] Estimates are based on preliminary information assembled by FPC staff in connection with work in updating the National Power Survey. The staff of the Water Pollution Control Administration in the Department of the Interior, in reviewing the data, suggests that the number of plants requiring cooling towers may be greater than the FPC staff estimate.

Hearings, Senate Subcommittee on Air and Water Pollution

February 27, 28, 1969; March 3 and 10, 1969; May 20 and 23, 1969; June 4, 1969

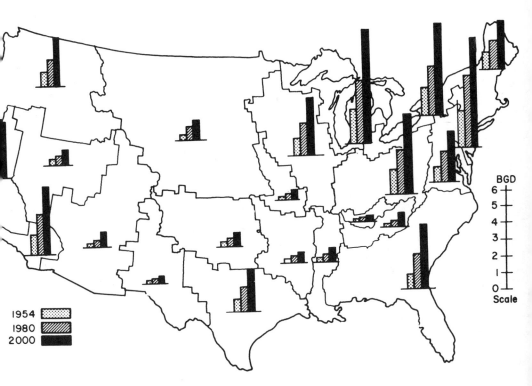

Projected Total Water Use from Municipal Systems — Billion Gallons a Day
"Waste Management and Control"—National Academy of Sciences 1966

Ground water is being depleted in many areas. For instance, in southern Arizona, ground water has been withdrawn for irrigation at such
high rates that the ground water level is over 230 feet below what it
was. As a result the land in areas is fissuring suddenly and caving in.
To compensate for this depletion, farmers and many politicians now
want to bring in Colorado River water which will salinate the land and
probably the ground water as well. Pumping of ground water in the
higher plains of Texas has completely exhausted the supply. On Long
Island, the depletion of ground-water supply is permitting seawater
and water from cesspools and sewage systems to leach directly into
water sources.

Estimated Total Withdrawals, Consumptive Uses and Returns to Streamflow
(Billions of gallons daily)

	1954			2000		
Use	Gross Withdrawal	Consumptive Use	Return	Gross Withdrawal	Consumptive Use	Return
Irrigation	176.1	103.9	72.2	184.5	126.3	58.2
Municipal	16.7	2.1	14.6	42.2	5.5	36.7
Manufacturing	31.9	2.8	29.1	229.2	20.8	208.4
Mining	1.5	0.3	1.2	3.4	0.7	2.7
Steam-Electric Power Cooling	74.1	0.4	73.7	429.4	2.9	426.5

Notes:

Withdrawals and consumptive uses from Report of the Select Committee on National Water Resources, 86th Congress, January 30, 1961.

Total estimated streamflow - 1,100 billion gallons daily.

"Waste Management and Control"—National Academy of Sciences 1966

WORLD HIGHWAY CONSTRUCTION EXPENDITURES

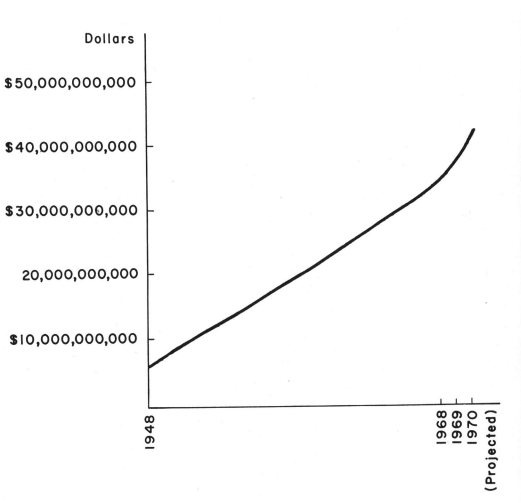

Source: THE NEW YORK TIMES December 26, 1969.

Traveling 600 miles, an automobile consumes as much oxygen as a human being consumes in a year.

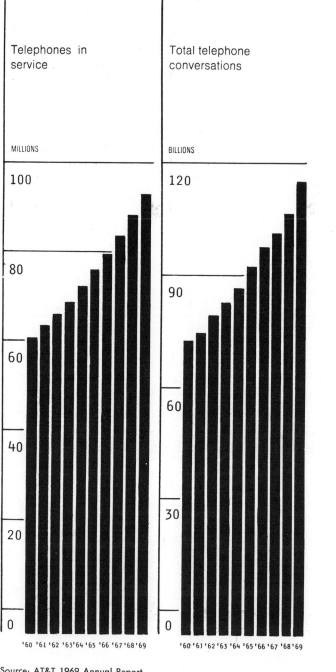

Telephones in service

MILLIONS

100

80

60

40

20

0

'60 '61 '62 '63 '64 '65 '66 '67 '68 '69

Total telephone conversations

BILLIONS

120

90

60

30

0

'60 '61 '62 '63 '64 '65 '66 '67 '68 '69

Source: AT&T 1969 Annual Report.

75% of the interstate circuit mileage we

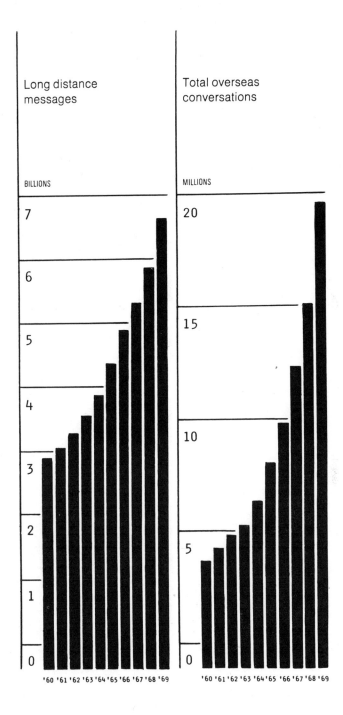

Long distance
messages

Total overseas
conversations

BILLIONS

MILLIONS

will require by 1980 remains to be built.

PEOPLE USING 32 UNITED STATES NATIONAL PARKS

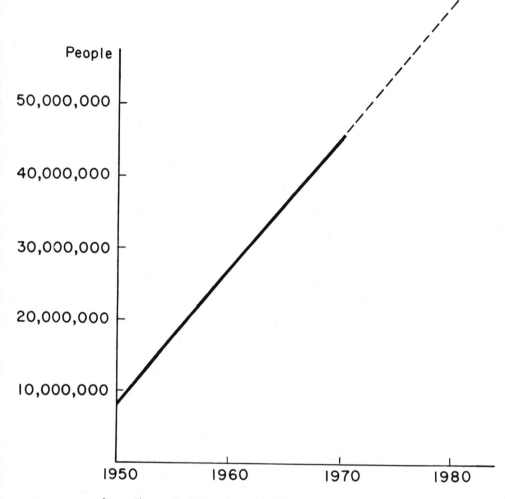

Source: The New York Times, September 1, 1969.

The national parks are severely overcrowded. They have a 7% annual growth rate in visitation. There are 4 times as many people in the parks as there were 20 years ago: 42,000,000 people at 32 parks of 27 million combined acres. In 1968 3000 people went through the Grand Canyon on the Colorado River. In 1969 10,000 people made the same trip. Serious crime in the national parks rose 67.6% in 1968, compared with 16% for the country.

In early 1970, the United States Army stockpiled chemical and biological warfare materials in the following known places:

Edgewood Arsenal, Edgewood, Maryland
Blue Grass Army Depot, Richmond, Kentucky
Anniston Army Depot, Anniston, Alabama
Pine Bluffs Arsenal, Pine Bluffs, Arkansas
Pueblo Army Depot, Avondale, Colorado
Rocky Mountain Arsenal, Denver, Colorado
Tooele Army Depot, Tooele, Utah
Umatilla Army Depot, Hemiston, Oregon

The Rocky Mountain Arsenal had about 12,000 tons of GB nerve gas and 5,000 tons of mustard gas.

The Army states that it sold all its phosgene gas, about 7,730,000 lbs. or 3865 tons, to Jones Chemical Co. of Caledonia, New York, and Chemical Commodities, Inc., of Olathe, Kansas, for $106,695 in the summer or fall of 1969. On August 15, 1969, 15 tons of this phosgene gas mistakenly arrived by rail in Buffalo, New York and sat in the rail yard unattended for 24 hours. During this time there was a serious collision of other rail cars 150 feet from the cars carrying phosgene.

In October 1969, the United States Army admitted that its nerve gas had caused a massive sheep kill in Utah several months earlier. Some 20 lbs. of nerve gas killed about 6,000 sheep. The accident, according to the Army, cost about $1 million: $371,685 for reimbursement for the sheep; $198,300 for temporary loss of contaminated land; and $464,850 for investigations and lab fees to see what killed the sheep.

A rough tabulation of some of the pelts offered for sale for ten months during 1968-69, as reported by Women's Wear Daily.

178,656	red foxes
43,931	white foxes
107,381	raccoons
881,614	squirrels
4 to 5 million	muskrats
774,287	beavers
17,915	otters
540,000	seals taken from the Gulf of St. Lawrence alone
85,782	wild mink
64,481	lynx
23,702	prairie wolves
4,350	timber wolves—an endangered species
7,104	fishers
2,490	badgers
2,996	black and brown bears
79	polar bears—an endangered species
28,700	marten—becoming scarce
94,488	opossums
510	leopards

During the winter of 1969, Gina Lollobrigida, the Italian film actress, wore a tiger skin maxicoat in London. She was publicly criticized for wearing a coat which took 10 skins to make: the world population of tigers is just 600. Replying to the criticism, Miss Lollobrigida said: "Might as well stop killing chickens for meat."

U.S. POPULATION GROWTH, GNP AND ENERGY CONSUMPTION [1]

Year	Population (millions)	GNP (billions $)	Per Capita GNP ($)	Anthracite	Bituminous coal, lignite	Crude Petroleum [2]	Natural Gas	Electricity [3]	Total Energy
1930	123.1	90.4	734	1,718	11,921	5,652	2,212	—	21,503
1940	132.6	95.0	716	1,245	11,290	7,487	2,969	—	22,911
1950	152.3	263.3	1,729	1,013	11,900	12,706	6,933	—	32,552
1960	180.7	495.2	2,740	447	9,967	18,608	14,163	1,631	44,816
1968	201.2	822.6	4,088	262	13,142	24,629	21,757	2,474	62,264

[1] In trillions of BTUs. Except for Alaskan bituminous coal, Alaska and Hawaii are not included in the energy totals until 1960.

[2] Beginning 1950, consumption includes petroleum products (net imports).

[3] Hydropower and nuclear power converted to coal input equivalents at prevailing average pounds of coal per kilowatt hour each year at central electric plants.

Sources: SPECIAL ANALYSIS OF THE BUDGET OF THE UNITED STATES 1970, Bureau of the Budget; STATISTICAL ABSTRACT OF THE UNITED STATES 1969, U.S. Department of Commerce.

Population Reference Bureau February 1970

In American firms, one of every twenty employees is an alcoholic. Many firms are starting their own rehabilitation programs. There are 7,000,000 alcoholics in the country. 300,000 of these are members of Alcoholics Anonymous. Only 3% of the country's alcoholics are on Skid Row. The fastest rising group of alcoholics is housewives. The ratio used to be one alcoholic woman to eight alcoholic men; now it is one woman to three men.

HONEY BEE POPULATION IN ARIZONA

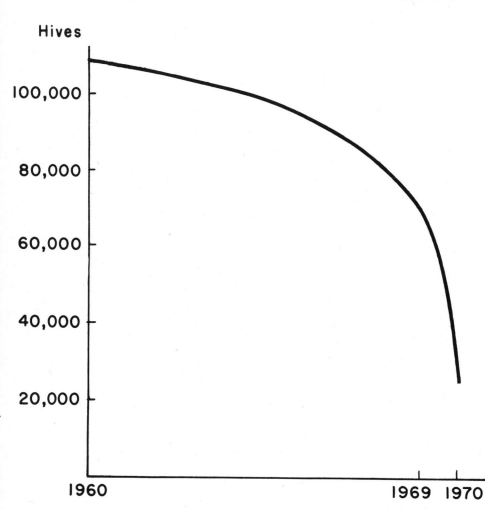

Source: ARIZONA REPUBLIC December 14, 1969.

The decline is apparently due to pesticides used as substitutes for DDT. The destruction of honey bees threatens the crops: melons, cucumbers, citrus and cotton.

It has been said that if human beings were to be sold over the counter for food, they would be impounded by the Department of Agriculture for failing to meet Federal standards regarding contamination from pesticides and other toxic substances.

FACTS ABOUT "TANKERS"

Pollution of waterways by oil is almost a normal occurrence in the operation of tankers and other cargo ships.

Oil spills occur when fuel lines are connected or disconnected, when bilge water or oily ballast is pumped out, when tanks overflow. In confined waterways such as harbors, these repeated spillages have resulted in continuous, chronic oil pollution.

The threat of a major oil spillage on the British Columbia or Arctic coast will become more acute with the tanker traffic which will result from the oil discoveries in Alaska and the MacKenzie delta.

In the three years prior to the grounding of the TORREY CANYON on the southwest tip of England, tankers were involved in an average of two collisions per week throughout the world. Over the past ten years, American registered tankers have been involved in an average of one collision per week, and in almost ten percent of these collisions oil pollution was a threat.

The size of new supertankers is such that an accident involving their oil being spilled would be a major catastrophe on the coast. The TORREY CANYON had a capacity of 115,000 tons of oil and the MANHATTAN is a similar size. There are now over 200 tankers of 200,000 tons capacity on order or built, several tankers (such as the UNIVERSE IRELAND) over 300,000 tons, and a 500,000-ton giant is being designed.

One thousand tons of oil would cover a 30-inch wide beach ½ inch deep in oil for a length of 20 miles. Oil spilled in water changes over time, with the lighter fractions evaporating over the first few days. It forms various oil-in-water emulsions and water-in-oil emulsions and after a period of months bacterial action will oxidize all but 10-15% of the oily mass, the 10-15% which remains accounts for most of the oily blobs that get washed onto beaches or caught in nets.

The technology of cleaning up oil slicks is very primitive, soaking it in straw or sawdust and then burning the straw.

Source: Canadian Scientific Pollution and Environmental Control Society.

Approximately 700 million tons of petroleum products pollute the seas every year. Of this total, 420 million tons is crude oil. Petroleum products and crude oil get into the sea from pumping, shipwrecks, loading and unloading operations, and from oil well spills and blowouts. Shipping losses for 1968 were:

    91 ships foundered
     9 ships missing
    51 ships burned
    23 ships in collisions
   142 ships wrecked
    10 ships lost in other causes

SIGNIFICANT SPILLS AND POTENTIAL SPILLS FROM VESSELS NOV. 1, 1968, TO JAN. 24, 1969

Location	Vessel	Company	Material quantity	Waters affected	Comments
Cincinnati, Ohio, Ohio River	Barge in tow of MV Nelson W. Broadfoot.	Ingram Barge Line	Gasoline, 12,000 gallons	Ohio River Markland Pool.	Spilled material evaporated.
Rehobeth Beach, Del	Oil Barge Hess Hustler	Hess Oil Co	No. 6 fuel ,1,000 gallons.	Delaware Bay	2 miles of beach contaminated. Oil soaked sand removed by convict labor and hauled to disposal site. Company payed and hauled to disposal site. Company payed for cleanup.
Rockaway Point, N.Y	Tanker Mary A. Whalen	Reliance Transfer Co	4,000 barrels No. 4 fuel	Atlantic Coast	Heavy storm caused grounding and loss of oil. Also dissipated spill.
St. Marks River, Fla	Oil Barge	Seminole Oil Co	9,000 gallons crude oil	St. Marks River Estuary	Marshes coated with oil and some smearing of pleasure craft. Company cleared one marina of oil.
Savannah, Ga	Tanker Texaco South Carolina.	Texas Co	Asphalt, 1,400 barrels	Savannah River	Asphalt solidified and sent to river bottom.
Block Island, R.I	Oil Barge	Moran Towing Co	Oil	Long Island Sound	Beaches contaminated in spots from Watch Hil Point to Point Judith. Company agreed to cleanup Connecticut beaches (1.5 miles).
Algiers Canal, La	Qil Barge Sally'O	Louis S. Breaux Towing Co.	300 barrels distillate	Mississippi River	Mississippi River covered by oil slick. Booms not practical due to strong currents. Dissipated by evaporation and currents.
Carrolton Bend, New Orleans, La	Oil barge	Union Transportation Co.	2,500 barrels No. 6 fuel	Mississippi River	No action taken. Strong river currents precluded booming and oil dissipated without apparent damage.
Markland Pool, Cincinnati, Ohio	Probably barge		Slick, ½ mile by 60 feet.	Ohio River	Municipal water intakes closed as precautionary measure.
Buzzards Bay off Massachusetts	Tanker Algol	Chartered by Mobil	No. 6 fuel	Buzzards Bay	Small quantities spilled. Private salvor contracted to remove vessel and prevent pollution at company's expense.

Hearings, Senate Subcommittee on Air and Water Pollution February 27, 1969-June 4, 1969

SIGNIFICANT SPILLS FROM PIPELINE SHORE AND OFFSHORE INSTALLATIONS NOV. 1, 1968, TO FEB. 22, 1969

Location	Material	Quantity/source	Damages	Waters affected	Company responsible	Action taken
San Diego, Calif	Bunker C	42,000 gallons pipeline		San Diego Bay	San Diego	Dispersant applied company expense.
Westbrook, Maine	Chemical waste	Quantity unknown factory.	Not determined	Presumpscot River, Maine.	S. D. Warren Paper Co	None.
Bridgeport, Conn	No. 4 fuel	30,000 gallons transferred from barge to tank farm.	90 percent of Harbor covered by film of oil.	Bridgeport Harbor, Conn	Hoffman Fuel Co	Dispersant applied Company expense.
Fairhaven California Eureka	Gasoline diesel fuel mix	100,000 gallons pipe from storage tank.	Waterfowl killed, estimate 5,000.	Humboldt Bay, Calif	Standard Oil of California	None.
ICW, west of Morgan City, La	Crude oil	63,000 gallons pipeline	Pollution of Intercoastal Waterway.	Intercoastal Waterway, Louisiana.	Texas Pipeline Co	Boomed and skimmed by company.
Albany, N.Y.	Slop oil	100,000 gallons storage tank.	Not determined concealed by ice.	Meeker Kill, Hudson River, N.Y.	Sears Oil	Boom erected to absorb oil by company.
Richmond, Calif	Diesel fuel	10,000 gallons pipeline.	None reported	El Cerrito Creek.	Sante Fe Railroad	Boomed creek vacuum truck picked up oil by company.
Lima, Ohio	Light crude	100,000+ gallons pipeline.	Fires in residential areas, sewage treatment plant damaged	Ottawa River, Ohio	Buckeye Pipeline Co	Creek boomed and vacuumed by company.
Rochester, N.Y.	Gasoline	10,000 gallons spilled from storage tank.	None reported	Genesee River	Mobil Oil Co	Fire department flushed gasoline into sewers.
Peru, Ind.	J.P. 4	30,000 gallons storage tank.	Stream befouled	Deer Creek—Tributary of Wabash River.	U.S. Air Force, Greisham AFB.	Air Force personnel covered fuel with foam and flush it into stream.
Seattle, Wash.	Diesel fuel	90,000 gallons storage tank pump.	Private boats smeared, shoreside facilities oiled.	Lake Union, Wash.	Washington Natural Gas Co.	Adsorbents made available but not used. Fire department ordered use of dispersants. Company assumed costs.
Santa Barbara, Calif.	Heavy crude	3,000 barrels, offshore drilling (Feb. 4, 1969).	Beaches oiled, boats smeared, waterfowl distressed.	Santa Barbara Channel	Union Oil Co	Dispersants and adsorbents applied. Booms and skimmers used.
Providence, R.I.	No. 5 fuel oil	1,000 gallons storage tank overflow.	Slick in yacht harbor	Providence Harbor	U.S. Navy Reserve training center.	Rhode Island and Navy Reserve personnel cleaned up.

Hearings, Senate Subcommittee on Air and Water Pollution February 27, 1969-June 4, 1969

OIL WELL BLOW-OUT POTENTIALS IN THE SANTA BARBARA CHANNEL

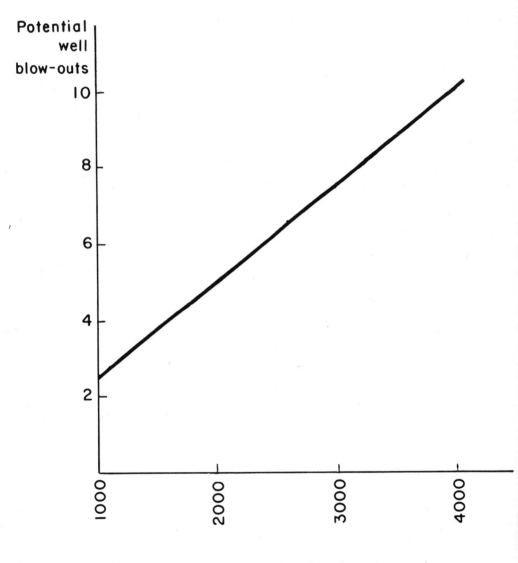

Source: New York Times Magazine 10/12/69

Pollution does not respect political boundaries. A huge American Smelting and Refining Co. smelter in El Paso, Texas, pours sulfur smoke into Juarez, Mexico. Acrid air from Central Europe is despoiling Norway: recently Norway and Sweden had a "black snow" because filthy, acrid air from the Ruhr in Germany was trapped by an inversion layer. Norwegian rivers show high acidity from sulfuric acid produced in England and Germany, mainly Germany. Norwegian forests are being stunted by polluted air from Central Europe.

By the middle of 1970, Los Angeles had already had 4 severe smog alerts that year. In the winter of 1969, an inversion layer lasted for 18 days in Phoenix and piled pollution 20,000 feet in the air. The summer of 1970 saw serious pollution along the whole East Coast.

In August of 1970, the New York City Department of Air Resources stated that during 1970, the city's air had been classified "unhealthy" in a little more than one day out of every four.

In 1969 the total budgets for state and local air-pollution control programs in the United States were $47 million: less than 25¢ per person per year. $15 per person per year was spent on solid waste control.

Bigger Cities ▶ More Air Pollution ▶ More Deaths

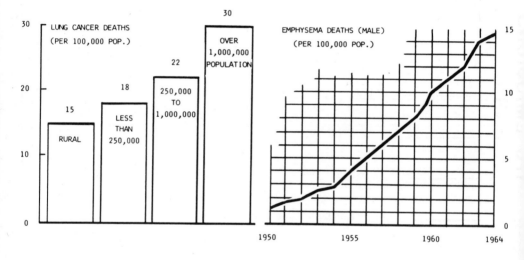

AIR POLLUTANTS   135 MILLION TONS PER YEAR

"A Strategy for a Livable Environment" publication of the Department of Health, Education and Welfare

higher levels of hydrocarbons...

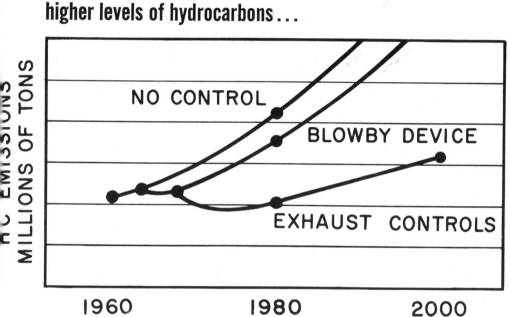

Source: Today and Tomorrow in Air Pollution, Public Health Service, Department of
Health, Education and Welfare

higher levels of sulphur dioxide...

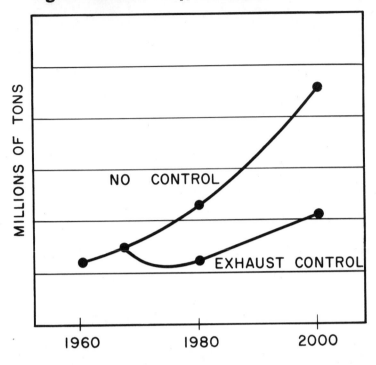

higher levels of carbon monoxide...

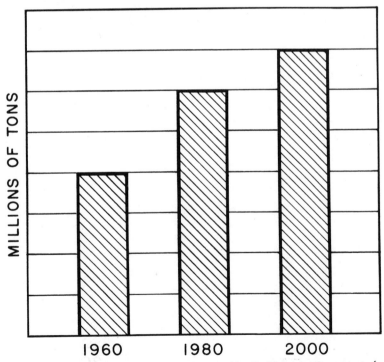

Source: Today and Tomorrow in Air Pollution, Public Health Service, Department of Health, Education and Welfare

higher levels of nitrogen oxides...

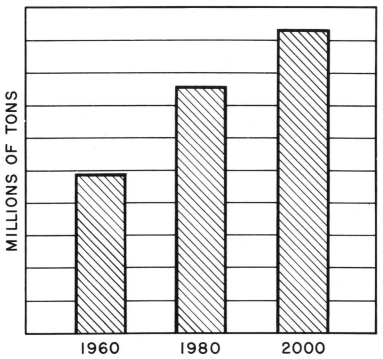

MILLIONS OF TONS

1960   1980   2000

higher levels of particulates...

MILLIONS OF TONS

1960   1980   2000

Source: Today and Tomorrow in Air Pollution, Public Health Service, Department of Health, Education and Welfare

Trains dump the following amounts of raw sewage on tracks yearly:

    30,000 locomotives and 15,000 cabooses dump
        30.5 million gallons of waste and
        61.5 million pounds of feces
    296 million passengers dump
        90 million gallons of waste and
        200 million pounds of feces
    Totals: 120.5 million gallons of waste yearly
             261.5 million pounds of feces yearly

Each year litter is deposited on the nation's highways at the rate of one cubic yard of trash per mile of every American highway. 59% of trash is paper goods. 16% is cans. 6% is plastic items, 13% is miscellaneous items from hair curlers to washing machines.

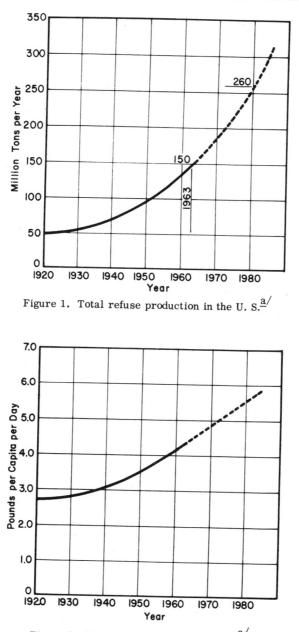

Figure 1. Total refuse production in the U. S.[a/]

Figure 2. Per Capita refuse production.[a/]

Figures 1 and 2 were prepared as part of a report to the Surgeon General's
Advisory Committee on Urban Health Affairs: Solid Wastes Handling in
Metropolitan Areas. Division of Environmental Engineering and Food Pro-
tection; Public Health Service; Department of Health, Education and Welfare,
February 1964. 41 p. multilithed.

National Academy of Sciences 1966

"Waste Management and Control"

RADIATION HAZARDS

SHIPMENTS OF RADIOACTIVE MATERIALS

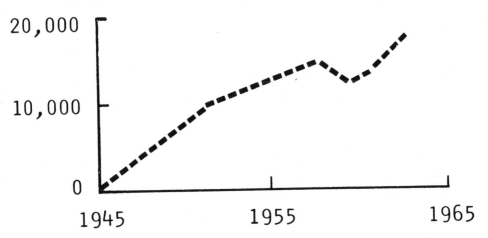

REACTOR WASTE PRODUCTION

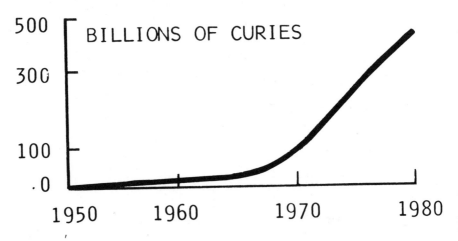

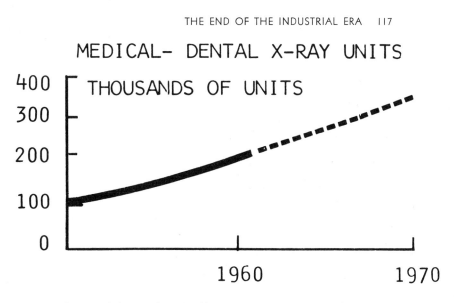

Source: "A Strategy for a Livable Environment." Department of
Health, Education, and Welfare.

Fifteen years ago in Grand Junction, Colorado, the American Metal
Climax Co. gave 300,000 tons of radioactive mine tailings to builders
for land fill under new housing developments. Now the tailings are
releasing radon gas, which comes from the breakdown of radium, and
the gas is seeping into the homes. The radioactivity level in some 3,000
homes is now above levels permitted in uranium mines.

The technique of presentation that we have adopted so far in this chapter has inherent limitations. We have tried to remind people of trends which are already visible. But this technique can only be used to state part of the message which needs to be conveyed.

The central reality which must be understood is that national and transnational systems are caught up in an uncontrolled and immensely rapid process of change. We must therefore try to state other types of change which are not yet so well known but which are nevertheless part of the overall pattern within which we are now living. We shall list some elements of this change process which are still little commented:

—Man's power and mobility are now so great that his actions inevitably cause unprecedented changes in ecological systems. For example, the World Health Organization, an agency of the United Nations, used DDT in Borneo to eliminate malaria-carrying mosquitoes. Mosquitoes were successfully killed. On the other hand, roaches survived and accumulated DDT. The geckoes, long-tailed lizards who are the natural predators of roaches, continued to eat them. The geckoes proved vulnerable to DDT accumulations and fell easy prey for cats. The DDT in the geckoes killed the cats. The loss of the cats made it possible for the rats to move in from the forest. The rats brought the threat of plague. New cats were parachuted in to kill the rats, which they did. The lack of geckoes, however, led to a further problem. They were also the natural predators of caterpillars which liked the roof thatching. The lack of the geckoes permitted the caterpillar population to explode, and the roofs fell in.

—In any ecological system, the gain or loss of one organism can have surprisingly extensive results. Major changes can develop if an external organism is introduced and finds a favorable ecological niche for its development. Some of the older, classic cases are the introduction of the rabbit into Australia and the introduction of the gray squirrel into England. Some newer cases:

In 1956 Professor Warwick Kerr, geneticist at Riberirao Preto School of Medicine, São Paulo, Brazil, imported 170 African killer-bee queens from Tanganyika. He wished to crossbreed these bees with local Brazilian bees. In 1956 Brazil was the world's third largest producer of honey, after Russia and the United States. In 1965 a workman left a door to the screened hive open, and twenty-six queens escaped. By 1967 Brazil was having to import honey, because swarms of killer bees were killing Brazilian bees. The bees also attack humans without provocation, and many people have been killed. The killer bees have spread to Argentina, Paraguay, Bolivia, and are entering Uruguay.

In 1964 a Florida fish dealer tired of buying exotic walking catfish from Southeast Asia. He tried to raise some in his own pond: the fish, however, ate his other fish, jumped out of the pond, and walked away. They have exploded all over Florida. They are a foot long, can walk for a quarter mile, and leave a lake which has been poisoned in order to kill them. They have caused many automobile accidents.

In 1966 a boy in Miami, Florida, brought back

three giant African snails from Hawaii as a present for his grandmother. They escaped, and in 1970 there were some 20,000 of them in a thirteen-block area. Big as a fist and a foot long inside the shell, the snails devoured foliage and even the paint of houses.

—An increasing number of manufactured products are noxious or dangerous. For example, male workers in a British birth-control-pill factory now wear space-age suits in order to avoid inhaling fumes which contain female hormones and which were causing the development of smooth skins and other female characteristics.

Manufactured goods must usually be transported from producers to destination. The danger inherent in the movement of weapons—whether high explosives or chemical/biological—have recently become obvious. There are also hazards, however, with "ordinary" products. These hazards can be expected to increase as the deterioration of railbeds and rolling stock continues. For example, in September 1969, an Illinois Central train derailed at Glendora, Mississippi, and four cars exploded. The cars were loaded with vinyl chloride, a chemical used in resins and plastics. This chemical decomposes into phosgene, a nerve gas, when overheated. All residents in a ten-mile radius were evacuated for twenty hours, and a twenty-five-mile radius was sealed off. Much livestock was killed.

—The density of population in various areas has risen rapidly. It is clear that the density is so high in some cases as to lead to a breakdown in community norms and values. While one cannot draw firm conclusions from parallels between experimental overcrowding of rats and real-life human situations, there are some highly uncomfortable similarities. The experiments of John Calhoun show that normal rat behavior breaks down totally under conditions of overcrowding. One can ask, therefore, if the growing self-destructive patterns in the ghetto are an inherent response to intolerable conditions.

The ghetto, however, is not the only example of overcrowding. It is clear that an increasing number of people find urban—and suburban—life intolerable. There is a growing rush to the rural areas, which is made possible by the growth of the mobile-home industry. Major migrations, however, always raise massive new problems and possibilities: economic and political patterns will necessarily change under the impact of new settlement patterns.

The mass migration may not be confined to those who can "afford" to move. The development of highly efficient agricultural machinery forced a large number of the poor off the land into the city. Any substantive program of welfare reform which equalizes benefits in the rural areas and in the cities would cause a substantial outflow as people went back to the country where they prefer to live. The change in political patterns, particularly in the South, would inevitably be dramatic.

—There has been a profound change in the position of all minorities. The development of effective communications has made it possible for minority groups to organize effectively **nationally**. The possibility of effective private **international** groups is just over the horizon. While the presence of effective communications has not been the only cause of the rapid growth of the movements for power and liberation, it has been an important contributing factor.

—The division of the world into abundance and scarcity regions has set up massive strains. A scientist from a scarcity region may be able to obtain three or four times as much money if he migrates to one of the abundance regions, compared to his salary if he stays in his own scarcity region. The same reality obtains for medicine. Hospitals in most large cities in the abundance regions would collapse if their foreign staff were removed. As brainpower and the capacity to move information effectively is now one of the prime determinants of development, it is clear that a vicious circle exists.

—Until recently, the fear about the future of the scarcity regions was that it was technically impossible to produce enough food to feed their people. It now appears that the Green Revolution may solve this problem. But the costs of the solution seem likely to be very high. Modern, effective agriculture is necessarily capital intensive and requires little labor. It must therefore be expected that as the Green Revolution spreads many people will be thrown out of work. There are no real answers at the present time as to what should be done with the displaced human beings.

During the process of industrialization in the abundance regions, the people released from farms were more or less effectively absorbed by mining and manufacturing, which then required large amounts of labor. Both of these sectors are now capital intensive, even in the scarcity regions. We therefore face an acute problem of unemployment and unemployability which cannot be dealt with by traditional means. If nontraditional means are not developed, massive social breakdown is inevitable.

—The inability to find technical solutions to the problem of hijacking is forcing countries toward a convention against air piracy. At first sight, such a technique appears likely to be fully successful. However, the attitudes of the Palestinian guerrillas, who can ignore the attitude of the Jordan government, shows that it will always be possible for a small group to act if it is prepared to ignore world public opinion. A group will ignore world public opinion if it is sufficiently desperate.

There is no practical or theoretical end to the listing of problems. Each exponential trend triggers other exponential trends in the systems around it. The effect of exponential trends in societies and ecosystems is therefore multiplicative instead of additive. The dangers are compounded because our linear mode of thinking ensures that problems remain largely invisible until they have developed to crisis proportions.

The multiplicative effect of exponential trends can be understood, for example, in terms of the effects of mixing chemicals in the human body. A particular medicine may be quite harmless when used by itself. However, it can become dangerous and even fatal if combined with another product. A commonly known danger is the effect of combining many drugs with alcohol.

We have essentially no knowledge at all about multiplicative effects within the human body, in socioeconomic systems, or in the ecosphere. But it is already possible to perceive some potentially relevant questions:

☐ Could cloud seeding to improve rainfall patterns in arid regions change world weather patterns, particularly when considered in the context of present alterations in solar penetration of the atmosphere resulting from growing pollution?

☐ Would melting the icecaps, either deliberately or as a result of unexpected weather modifications, drown coastal cities and alter existing patterns of sea life?

☐ Can the pollution of the ionosphere by rockets and supersonic aircraft significantly change the total weather picture of the earth?

☐ Have pesticide residues reduced the capacity of birds and other species to breed? If they do, will man have to devote vast resources to saving endangered species so as to preserve sufficient variation in the ecosphere?

☐ Has the level of radiation and chemicals in the human body already made sudden and frequent human mutations inevitable? Will attempts at planned genetic mutations in human beings improve or damage the human race? Do scientists have enough knowledge to carry out such tests "successfully"?

☐ Are there sufficient ways to get rid of industrial wastes and poisons? Or will they inevitably cause a breakdown—partial or total—in the world's biochemical composition?

☐ How will human beings react to the stress inherent in the shift from the industrial era to the cybernetic era? Do they have the capacity to survive the inevitable levels of stress? Will the adaptive techniques used by various groups—students, businessmen, unions, educators—be so contradictory as to cause total breakdown?

☐ Will the attempts of human beings to slow down the introduction of new technologies which threaten their jobs and their psychic security destroy the effectiveness of attempts to create change?

———

Some years ago, Barbara Ward coined a term for the world: "Spaceship Earth." This term has gained wide currency and has proved a successful way to teach people about limitations on the capacity of the environment. We have learned that we must recycle our wastes if we are to survive, because the absorptive capacity of the ecosystem is not as great as the amount of waste we can produce.

We now need to make our understanding more complete. To do so, we must understand that man inherited a world which was far from stable. Within geological history, the earth has been racked by fire and ice: it was created in great violence. Since the climate became more equitable, there has been greater continuity. However, the view from which many biologists and ecologists still work—that there is a particular set of organisms which belong for all time in a given ecological niche—is totally incorrect. Species have been created and have died out continuously throughout the earth's history.

☐ **The novelty of our present situation does not lie in the fact of change. It lies in the magnitude of change which man himself is able to create and**

**in the fact that man is able to screen himself from
feedback patterns which would normally affect him.**
Overexpansion by any other species results in a
rapid diminution of the food supply available to
the species. This in turn cuts back the numbers of
the species. Man, however, prevents immediate
feedback from his actions.

☐ **It is this capacity of man to create and continue
exponential trends for long periods which makes
him unique. But man has not escaped from the
environment. He cannot shield himself from feedback forever.** Man has delayed the day of reckon-
ing, but he has not eliminated it. We have now
reached, at this particular point in time, the moment when man must deal with the consequences
of his past "conquests" of nature, which have
eroded the basis of his continued survival.

The analogy we should use is highly distressing.
Bacteria provided with a perfect culturing medium
will grow at great speeds until they reach the capacity of the culture to support them. As they approach this capacity, their growth rate falls off, and
later the bacteria will die out unless provided with
a new culture. Similarly, man found the earth a
perfect basis for growth in his population and his
activities. He is now at the point where he must
decide whether to control his growth or to undergo
the fate of a bacteria colony.

We can usefully expand the analogy. The problem for mankind can be perceived if we imagine
the earth as a bacteria culture which has bred
many types of bacteria. Originally, there was so
much food that the colonies of bacteria grew unchecked. Now we are reaching the point where the
rapidly growing colonies of bacteria are trying to

feed in the same areas. Conflict is breaking out among those who need the same resources and also among those who find that the wastes of other colonies befoul their own eating areas. In addition, mutants within each colony are turning on the colony itself.

The analogy is highly distasteful but basically accurate. Man has been the maximally effective parasite on the earth. In the process he has destroyed many of the resources required for his long-run survival. It is inevitable that perception of this fact will lead to much turbulence and conflict. It is also inevitable that partial solutions aiming to eliminate one problem may well create another which is more serious.

_____

Science fiction contains many examples of unexpected and unwanted byproducts of future trends. A few examples are given here:

☐ The growing potential effectiveness of machine systems threatens individuals with loss of their income and their sense of purpose. In order to preserve their dignity, men try to prevent machine systems and technology from being used. In so doing they prevent the development of the information and efficiency required to permit man to solve his problems.

☐ Western economic systems require that people buy all the goods which the society is capable of turning out. This, in turn, requires that tastes rise continuously. Such a goal can only be achieved in a commercial environment. One science-fiction story suggests that in the future the powerless will be forced to consume while the powerful will be able to enjoy spare time.

☐ Attempts to clean up sewage may well concentrate on only part of the problem and thus create new problems. Present patterns of waste-disposal planning threaten to increase the nutrients in the water so greatly as to lead to explosive growth in algae which will choke rivers and streams.

☐ So long as production is not integrated up and down the line—so long, in other words, as we preserve the concept of waste—solutions to pollution and solid wastes will always be partial and incomplete. All too often proposed solutions merely trade off one form of pollution for another: from land to air, from water to land. Indeed, "pollution control" often means simply making a particular pollutant invisible. For example, a massive oil slick from a blownout Chevron oil well off the Louisiana coast in early 1970 was treated with chemicals to make it sink underwater. Apparently the company believed that a slick which could not be seen would not be considered important. Similarly, some companies, including steel companies, are pouring waste industrial chemicals into deep wells—deep in the earth where they may seep into water supplies.

It is at this point that the individual reader must make up his mind. He must determine whether he believes that Dennis Gabor is right when he says that "It is only in mathematics that exponential curves grow to infinity. In real life they either saturate gently or they break down catastrophically. It is our duty as thinking men to strive toward a gentle saturation."

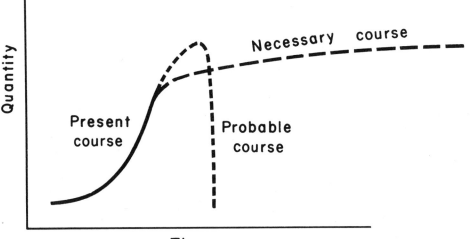

If Gabor is right, we must create a total change in our patterns of organization and thinking. The present industrial era **requires** continued exponential rates of growth. It **cannot exist** without them. This reality is most easily seen in economics, but it also controls all our other sociopolitical systems. A decision to strive toward a gentle saturation rather than to continue to promote exponential growth means the end of present thinking patterns and the development of totally new ones based on sapiential authority rather than structural authority.

There can be no justification for giving up the patterns of the industrial era unless it is quite clear that we are forced to do so. The risks involved in changing from one method of ordering society to another are enormous. We must only make the shift if it is absolutely necessary.

We do already know that human beings and ecosystems cannot survive exponential rates of change. Those who argue that we must adapt to ever-increasing rates of change are therefore profoundly incorrect. They are asking human beings and ecosystems to do the impossible.

From this point forward in this volume it will be assumed that the patterns of the industrial era are indeed nonviable. As a consequence, the methods of thinking and standards of proof used will change, for the book will be based on systemic thinking. The remainder of this volume will assume that the survival of man and the earth are only possible on the basis of a fundamental change in our ways of thinking and acting.

However, before considering how to move into the communications era, it seems useful to look once more at the process by which the industrial era developed. The intermission is designed to fulfill this purpose.

INTERMISSION. *TWO ERAS: ONE DYING, THE OTHER STRUGGLING TO BE BORN*

We stated at the end of the last chapter that the reader must be prepared to believe in the coming of a new era, at least temporarily, if he is to understand the rest of the book. Such a leap is, of course, extremely difficult, for it requires the abandonment of the principles which we have learned to employ in our models of thinking and patterns of action.

This intermission is therefore designed to show why new patterns of thinking and action are essential. It will consider the changes in world view during the development of the industrial era and sketch the basic nature of the new world view which must now emerge.

The success of the industrial era resulted from the fact that a linear mode of thinking was effectively developed. People decided what they wanted to accomplish and were not concerned with either the indirect or the long-term consequences of their actions. The fundamental organizing principle of the industrial era was a structural principle: those with authority had a right to command those placed lower down the line. The orders of those in authority were not to be questioned or disputed.

Structural authority and linear thinking are deeply compatible. Indeed they fitted together so well that they dominated the entire socioeconomy of the industrial era. In particular, linear thinking came to control intellectual activities. Scientists, economists, theologians, anthropologists, and historians shared the assumption that the world operated in a linear fashion. Linear thinking permitted disciplines to ignore all developments which were not directly related to their subject matter.

In America, and to a lesser extent in Europe, the full power of the linear, industrial mode was channeled into fulfilling one simple goal: increasing the production and consumption of ecofacts. The industrial era proved that linear thinking is extremely effective in producing excessive amounts of ecofacts. Up to the present time, the productive power of the industrial system has continuously been underestimated by those who thought they could predict its rate of growth.

The implications of the success of the industrial system are now becoming clear. The industrial era requires the existence of exponential trends in every area of life. Exponential trends are inherently uncontrollable and eventually fatal.

The last chapter demonstrated some of the perceived exponential trends in water use, energy use, poison buildups, and land despoilage. It also pointed out that in addition to the perceived trends, there are large numbers of equally dangerous trends which are still hidden. The most dangerous trends of all are those which are inherently unrecognizable, because we persist in a linear mode of thinking. These are the trends which stem from mulitiplicative interactions of various new developments: the recent unexpected discovery of high concentrations of mercury in fish is an example of the surprises which are inevitable in coming years. At this point we can only guess what trends may develop in the future because we lack a systematized means of examining them. It is important that we learn, for instance, about the effects, if any, of ionospheric pollution from rockets and jet aircraft on wheat production in Kansas and weather conditions in Ceylon. We must also develop means to discover the implications of the Green Revolution in Asia for the French peasant.

Examined without preconceptions, the industrial era must now be seen as a wildly oscillating, uncontrolled nonsystem. Present trends in America and the abundance regions are clearly out of control. Most trends have been growing at exponential rates. The society is moving into instability— instability of a kind which is certain to lead to total cultural/ ecological collapse if not corrected.

These assessments of our present situation parallel the dominant currents of opinion. Most Americans believe that something is wrong with their society, and they fear its disintegration. There is today considerable agreement about the seriousness of the situation.

However, it is very difficult for those brought up within the concepts of the industrial era fully to understand the reality of instability. We grew up with the belief that man was learning to control and dominate a wider and wider range of natural phenomena and that the possibility of unexpected events or dangerous instabilities was declining because of man's increasing power.

Why do industrial-era scholars hold this view? They examine the industrial era in terms of itself. They see the power generated by man's growing control over parts of nature and over his fellowmen. Few of them perceive either the secondary or the long-run consequences of this control— they are therefore convinced of the possibility of stability. Those scholars, such as Joseph Schumpeter, who *did* see the destabilizing implications of the industrial era at an early date were largely ignored.

Once one looks at the industrial era from the outside, we can easily see that its actions promote instability. Indeed, it is this reality which explains the rapid development of an understanding of the environmental crisis. The apparent stability within which people have perceived reality for so long is dissolving and is being replaced by a feeling of instability.

We must now act as though all systems are in flux. Because of the extent and magnitude of continuing change, we cannot afford to let any trend get out of control, for its impact on other instable trends may be multiplicative.

Changing world views

We are used to considering history in terms of people and dramatic events. In this intermission we shall look rather at the world views which have controlled our thinking and the changes which are now taking place.

John Maynard Keynes stated: "In the long run, it is ideas and not men which rule the world." The ways men act and think stem from their perceptions of reality. If one's perception of the nature of reality changes, so does one's action patterns.

We have already stated that one governing image of the industrial era was the watch. The idea of society as a watch spread deeply into all thinking. It was argued that economic, social, and political systems would operate effectively if people would act in their own self-interest. The free-market philosophy was an expression of this view in economics; the utilitarian calculus was an expression of this view in politics.

We are now so used to the perversion of this doctrine that we are in danger of forgetting that it was based on an understanding of one of the two critical aspects of ecological theory. The fact that people and other organisms were most capable of making decisions for themselves had been understood; the fact that this required a far better educated and more responsible society was largely ignored, except by a few writers such as John Stuart Mill.

As we try to create the society we need today, we must deal effectively with the second requirement. It is clear that structural authority cannot be effective in today's conditions. We must therefore develop sapiential authority. Sapiential authority, however, will not be possible without a rapid increase in the levels of wisdom and responsibility of the population of the world.

The failure to recognize the full implications of invisible-hand doctrines has been a primary cause of the intellectual movements—and political actions—of the last hundred years. We have tried to shore up, with increasing desperation, an intellectual doctrine which made less and less sense. The original idea that *responsible* men could most effectively manage their *own* affairs without outside interference degenerated until we came to believe that systems would be self-corrective even if nobody took responsibility for intelligent decision making.

During the nineteenth century, affairs were sufficiently simple that policy could be largely based on the belief that the government which governs least governs best. Undesirable developments were left to work themselves out: the cost in misery was considered unavoidable. Power and force were the ultimate arbiters of most major decisions.

This philosophy of government still has many adherents in the West—particularly in America. It is often argued that if only the government would stop getting into issues which did not concern it, our present problems would be greatly diminished. There is a nostalgia for the simplicity of the past which prevents many from coming to grips with the reality of today.

The early twentieth century

The freedom to use force and power in the nineteenth century produced such major imbalances that it was impossible to continue to operate on the same basis. No fundamental reconceptualization of the role of government took place, however: the society was still seen essentially as a watch. It was admitted, at this time, that the watch could go wrong from time to time and that a watch repairer—the government—should put it right. The design of the watch was not to be changed.

Governments therefore came to deal with problems as they arose. It was believed that there was no necessity to cope with the wider causes of the problems: consideration of possible secondary effects was inherently excluded because it was assumed that the watch would continue to run as before.

This style of government continued into the thirties. Policies in the Great Depression were still primarily based on the desire to reconstitute the economic, social, and political system of earlier periods. The style of the thirties was interventionist, but the purpose was to ensure the survival of a system that had worked well.

The forties, fifties, and sixties

It was nevertheless the intellectual agreements and the policy developments of the thirties which made the watch analogy impossible. Western countries came out of the Second World War with a commitment to full employment. Given the pace of increase in population and the inevitability of productivity increases, it became clear that intelligent government had to be based on the certainty of growth.

Once again, however, no major reconceptualization of the role of government took place. It became assumed that government had to deal with a situation in which the watch would inevitably grow into a clock. The problems facing the government were seen in terms of growth, not change. Rules of thumb inherited from earlier periods were used without any consideration of the need for new patterns of thought. The well-proved fact that a change in quantity eventually leads to changes in quality was ignored.

The lack of any real reconceptualization has meant, of course, that many observers and many politicians are still acting in terms of earlier patterns. A few are still trying to govern least. Many are still trying to keep the watch operating. Only a few have adapted fully to the growth theory—and they have reached the point of commitment to it just when it is becoming clear that the theory is no longer valid.

In the years since the Second World War, techniques developed which permitted an examination of the implications of continuous growth. We became expert, as a society, in determining how large the car population or the human population would become on the basis of extrapolations of present trends. Having made these calculations, we acted in ways which would permit present trends to continue to develop.

The extrapolist group has been responsible for an increasing amount of the thinking and action of recent years. Its work is based on the assumption that there will be no fundamental break between the past and the foreseeable future. A recent highly popular version of the extrapolists' view has been Alvin Toffler's book *Future Shock*. The message of his book can be simply summarized. The United States must expect massive change. However, this change results from the same forces which created American society in the first place. Man's desire to dominate the earth through understanding its constituent parts is still effective. Science and technology are still in control, and the results of developments in these fields will continue to determine the way we live. Toffler suggests that we are moving into a period of super-industrialism. He argues that, although the details of our socioeconomic landscape may alter, the nature of the landscape will remain the same.

The extrapolists' thinking is fully conveyed by the phrase the "super-industrial age." This phrase is formed by exactly the same process as the term "the horseless carriage." The initial car was created by putting an engine where the horse had been. There was no fundamental consideration of the nature of the motorcar, still less of the automobile. This came later and was only achieved by a costly process of trial and error rather than an initial conceptualization.

At the present time, the extrapolists are following the same process. It is assumed that the future will be like the past in general outline. It is admitted that there will be some removals of old patterns (by analogy the horse), but the new patterns which will replace them (by analogy the motor) are not perceived. Extrapolists see the displacement but not the addition.

The extrapolists argue that the future can be described

as an extension of present trends. Despite the apparent complexity of their process of analysis, their conclusions are drawn from linear thinking. It is assumed that the various trends of today will not conflict with each other and that none of the trends presently running will bring about fundamental changes in the motivations of the human beings who create these trends.

The extrapolist doctrine has some implications which are far from obvious at first sight. It is assumed that the trends of the industrial era will continue for an indefinite period. It is known, however, that these trends were based on certain institutional styles. The credibility of extrapolist thinking therefore comes to rest on the degree to which industrial-era institutions remain in existence.

In this period when intellectuals and politicians are so closely interrelated, it is a short step from basing one's predictions on the *assumption* that industrial-era values will continue to take steps to ensure that they will, in fact, continue. Increasingly, therefore, extrapolists are recommending that we reinforce industrial-era family, school, business, etc., styles. They are also attempting to prevent the creation of new communication-era institutions which would eventually replace industrial-era institutions.

The reactionary period through which we are now passing stems directly, therefore, from the dominant philosophy of recent years. We still assume as a society that growth within present patterns is inherently desirable. *In order to permit growth within present patterns, we must ensure that existing institutions remain viable and that new institutional styles which might challenge present institutions and values do not develop.*

In effect, it was the extrapolist doctrine which dominated the 1970 electoral campaign. The Nixon Administration attempted to convince the "silent majority of middle Americans" that America is moving in basically the right directions and that it is therefore appropriate to be intolerant of all forms of fundamental dissent. It used the work of the positive extrapolators such as Herman Kahn, Daniel Bell, and those in various government departments to justify the political approach. Inevitably, of course, this rhetoric was also found appealing by those who believe that the government is best which governs least.

This reality has been widely commented. However, it is not recognized that the fundamental disagreement with the policies of recent and present Administrations stems from the *same* world view. The radicals of the sixties *also* believed in the extrapolist view, but instead of thinking that it was desirable for present trends to continue, they argued that extended continuation of present societal directions would be disastrous. Both the positive extrapolators and the radicals believed that existing trends were unchangeable—their view of the desirability of this situation was at opposite poles.

The radicals behaved as they did because they believed that they were justified in doing anything which might arrest the juggernaut of present trends: they tried to tear down all existing structures. If they had had any real belief that the world could change for the better, they would have been interested in creating rather than destroying.

The year 1970 marked the point at which the power of the extrapolists was broken. Perhaps the most dramatic evidence to support this apparently extreme statement is an editorial in the June 1970 issue of *Fortune*—a magazine little given to extreme statements—which argues that the degree of breakdown in the norms of American life is now so great that the survival of the United States as a viable entity can no longer be assumed.

> For the first time, it is no longer possible to take for granted that the U.S. will somehow survive the crisis that grips it. The land itself will survive, of course, along with the machines and the people—or most of them. But no nation is merely, or mainly, an aggregate of its geography, its material assets, and its warm bodies. At the core of the U.S., conferring identity, cohesion, and vital-

ity stands a Proposition: freemen, despite differences of status, belief, and interest, can govern themselves. Upon the survival of that Proposition, confirmed by eight generations of superb achievement, depends any worthwhile future that an entity called the United States might have. And it is that Proposition—amazingly— which in the spring of 1970 has come to be at stake.

The late sixties and early seventies

The sudden decline in acceptance of the views of the extrapolators produced a vacuum which had to be filled. It is no longer possible to argue convincingly that trends are inevitable. A reaction is therefore taking place, and many in the United States are swinging to the opposite extreme. Today, the popular view argues that we can invent a future without constraints from the past. It will be convenient to call this group creatists.

The extent of the dominance of this new view is shown by the phenomenal success of *The Greening of America*, by Charles Reich. His volume argues that a new life-style is coming into existence and that this new life-style will—in and of itself—change America.

Creatists believe that we cannot allow past trends to determine our future. They argue, in effect, that we cannot permit the industrial era to continue, that fundamental changes in all our socioeconomic systems are immediately necessary.

Creatists usually have some primitive visions of the possible alternatives to the industrial system. They argue that we must develop totally different patterns for individuals, nations, and the world. They claim that new patterns will lead us to invent new life-styles which will enable us, as individuals and communities, to live within the limitations of our environment.

The essential heart of the creatist view is the belief that a new culture can be created without influence from the industrial era. Creatists believe that the past does not have to influence the future. They believe that there are no real constraints on what they can do. For them the process of socioeconomic change is merely a matter of "do it."

Many social activists, reformers, and ex-liberals have adopted the creatist view. So have many of the ecology groups, many of those in the religious revival, and much of the new party politics. The term "counterculture" is sometimes used to classify the creatists.

The creatists have moved part—but not all—the way toward systemic thinking. In terms of the analogy used earlier, they analyze not the removal of the horse but rather the addition of the motor: they do not, however, perceive the total new system as an automobile.

Very often they diagnose past and present trends accurately. For example, they usually perceive that the poor can have little control over their lives. They perceive that the society is not moving rapidly enough to meet the needs of today. They perceive that people are failing to use their abilities to make changes which are essential. Typically, creatists understand that an indefinite expansion of industrial-era patterns can only lead to disaster for America and the world. They perceive that industrial societies must find ways to alter their behavior patterns so that they work within environmental limitations.

The creatists understand that our only hope for survival on this planet is to create a fundamentally different culture. They also move a further step and take action in the light of what they understand about the world today. They attempt to employ their new awareness to create communities and organizations which will ensure the survival and attractive development of the world. These people *are* attempting to create a world which they find attractive. They appear to many, therefore, to be initiators of a new culture which is based on systemic thinking.

The failure of the creatists arises precisely from the fact that they believe that they can create a new culture without being influenced by the industrial era. Instead of making the valid point that the past *need not determine* the future when alternative choices are intelligently presented, they claim that the past will not influence the future.

The experience of many communes and ecology groups illustrates the pattern of the creatists. Communes often start from the insight that society blocks messages and ideas which it does not wish to hear. In order to avoid this pattern, the commune then makes a rule that all members must be open to all messages. This rule is designed to overcome the destructive blocking of messages that occurs in industrial bureaucracies.

The rule fails to recognize that complete openness is impossible. The survival of the human being depends on complex screens which order reality into patterns which the individual can handle. Demanding that an individual be open to all messages all the time therefore creates an impossible overload condition.

Communes which permit overload conditions to develop cease to work effectively. Ironically, they are then forced to behave exactly like overloaded linear organizations: they resort to rhetoric instead of communication, and they are unable to hear new ideas which could break them out of the vicious circle of overload. Failing to perceive the necessity of screening systems, many communes tend to develop unperceived screens which make them ingrown and dysfunctional. They become as sterile as any linear group.

There is evidence that those who have tried to develop functioning new communities are learning this lesson. More and more communes are closed to casual visitors. More and more groups are developing complex screening patterns in order to determine whether people who wish to join the community will be compatible with present members. Communities are discovering the necessity for a shared community myth.

Many ecology groups also illustrate the pattern of the creatists, for example the evolution of Environmental Action, the group which coordinated Earth Day, April 22, 1970. This group was originally intended as an information clearing house for the activities of ecology groups around the country. In the end, Environmental Action ended up behaving like an industrial-era organization: it sought to build a power base, it apparently felt justified in suppressing vital information, and it even attempted to dictate policies and actions to local groups.

The original idea was attractive: small groups of people thinking systemically would benefit from hearing about each other's activities and progress. A communication system would therefore be helpful. However, the people who ran Environmental Action failed to perceive the real requirements of a communication system and the fundamental ways it differs from a control system. They therefore moved back from a system intended to facilitate communication to an organization seeking to ensure power.

The creatists believe that they have broken free of linear thinking. In fact, however, they inevitably move backward and end up reverting to the linear mode of thinking. Since systemic thinking is still in its infancy, we have not yet developed fully systemic action patterns. The only clear-cut patterns are those based on linear thinking—the creatists fall back into this old style on most occasions.

The effect of the creatists on society is therefore very often negative. The creatists have a highly divisive, fragmenting effect on the society. Because the creatists live on the basis of fragmentary and partial perceptions of who they are and what they do, they necessarily transfer their own fragmented patterns to the total society.

The developing pattern

We must now move beyond the creatists and meld their valid insights with those which are correct in the extrapolists' view. We must make a fundamental shift in our perspective.

This shift occurs when one ceases to perceive our present situation as a formless mass of shifting patterns which are out of control and instead begins to perceive the new patterns of stability and order which are still largely invisible but already forming. This shift overcomes the compulsion of

Americans to diagnose their problems and replaces it with the desire to discover new possibilities which can become solutions to our problems. Stated another way, the shift in perspective occurs when the desire to describe the dying industrial era gives way to the discovery of the new shoots of the future which are already with us but largely invisible.

There are many ways in which this fundamental shift in perspective can be triggered. One of the most common ways is for a person to recognize the real truth of the statement that we are living between two eras, one dying and the other struggling to be born. We are living at a time when the degenerative period of the industrial era and the developmental period of the communications era overlap.

The real magnitude of this shift in perspective can perhaps best be seen by looking at four of its immediate, critical implications.

First, one's comprehension of systemic thinking is always partial and incomplete. It is therefore essential to develop continuously one's understanding. The old saw "the more you know, the more you don't know" takes on increased validity. Having made a breakthrough in understanding present dynamics in America, it suddenly becomes clear how much the society must learn if America is to avoid total collapse. New levels of personal and societal skill are necessary.

Second, the principle of sapiential authority enables a person to order the world for himself. He comes to trust his own evaluations and his own desires. We must therefore cease to speak of anomie—the situation in which the individual is perceived as unable to find his place in a well-functioning society. Rather, we must use the idea of amondie—a situation in which the society is recognized as so poorly structured that it fails to provide meaningful opportunities for people living within it.

Third, a person tries to find others who will inform him of the mistakes he is making. Each person attempts to create feedback patterns which permit him to find out when he is acting unwisely. Those who move toward systemic thinking try to create environments for themselves in which they can be self-corrective. They recognize that working with those who already think systemically is the quickest way to learn.

Fourth, those who already have some experience in systemic thinking try to impart it as rapidly as possible to those who have just committed themselves to understanding systemic thinking. They know that each individual will contribute new insights as soon as he learns the basic patterns of systemic thinking.

Systemic thinking implies that people become self-directed. People make decisions for themselves. Sanctions are internalized by each individual instead of imposed externally by a bureaucracy. New stabilizing factors and new institutions are created. Instead of having stabilizing factors imposed externally, as in the structurally based industrial era, stabilizing factors are chosen and internalized according to the principles of sapiential authority.

A different culture will therefore emerge: it can conveniently be called the *communications era*. Previously we have called this era the cybernetic era. The cybernetic era was named from the concept that nonhuman feedback mechanisms were being created: the communications era describes the overall results of this addition.

What does it mean when we say that we must create a new culture? Previous cultures faced with radical instability attempted to treat the *symptoms* of change at work within them. These cultures met instability with repression and thereby brought on their own collapse. The experience of previous cultures demonstrates, therefore, that the attempt to regain stability by reestablishing old stabilizing factors— i.e., traditional institutions—is counterproductive. If a set of stabilizing factors has ceased to be effective, a new set is required. Creating a new set of stabilizing factors—new institutions—is the same as creating a new culture. The remainder of this volume will develop some of the implications of this new culture.

Toward viewing our possibilities

From this point on, we shall assume that systemic think-ing is essential. The book now moves away from examining our problems toward perceiving our possibilities. Up to this point, we have looked at the process by which the industrial era is inevitably moving toward total cultural/ecological col-lapse. We shall now be concerned with the process by which continued viability can be ensured. In effect, we shall discuss some of the essential steps in the process of building a new culture for the communications era.

The steps by which we can gain continued viability are essentially unprecedented. Precisely because our situation is ahistorical, there are no ready-made decisions for us to act on. We cannot benefit directly from those who have gone before us. Man's present repositories of knowledge cannot be assumed to be of direct help to us, for they are primarily organized in terms of the world view of the industrial era. Nor can adults say they have the answers because they have lived longer. No one can tell us what decisions we must make, because no one has trod the path we must tread. We must learn a new style of thinking and a new style of living. We must learn for ourselves.

These statements are not meant to devalue the philosophi-cal wisdom within the various intellectual traditions of the world. A reexamination of these traditions will probably show that Western man has lost touch with much of mankind's reservoir of wisdom as he moved into the industrial era. It remains true, however, that this wisdom is not widely avail-able at this point in time, nor can it provide *direct and immediate* answers to the questions we face today.

The challenge to the reader that he take up systemic thinking is not made lightly. To perceive possibilities is far more demanding than to examine problems. The task before us is one of building a new culture. While each person who decides to accept this task need bear only part of the total responsibility, a great deal which is unknown must be learned, and a large amount of what is now done must be abandoned.

In Chapter 6 we shall look at potential new positive factors. These new factors have been with us for some time, but they have been hidden by the bright-light effect of our obvious instability. The communications era which is struggling to be born has been hidden by the industrial era, which is dying ungracefully.

In Chapters 7 and 8 we shall look at techniques people can use to develop their understanding of the world. In Chapter 9 we shall discuss some of the new policies which can move us through the transition from the present disastrous course into the process of creating a new, dynamically stable society.

PART 2 THE COMING OF THE
COMMUNICATIONS ERA

CHAPTER 6 *THE REASONS FOR HOPE*

What is the nature of the shift in perspective that we must learn to practice? *If we continue to study the present in terms of past realities, it is inevitable that we shall only perceive decay and collapse.* If, on the other hand, we come to understand the principles which should organize our lives in the communications era, we shall find that the seeds of the future are already planted.

From this point on, we shall cease to study how and why the industrial era is decaying. Rather we shall search for indicators which show that the communications era is already successfully emerging. In order to achieve this new goal, we shall need to use a variety of teaching techniques. Experience shows that different people find different techniques of value to them.

This chapter will set out the nature of the new communications era in a relatively conventional essay form. A later chapter will use systemic techniques.

The effective uses of INTER

Earlier in this volume we introduced the concept of INTER, a logical communication style which permits us to draw correct conclusions when both the question to be answered and the existing conditions are known. Today, however, the use of INTER is often invalid because we need *either* to discover the relevant question *or* to perceive the existing conditions within the culture—in some cases we need to do both.

In effect, we have been using INTER in many inappropriate ways. We have tried to derive formally correct conclusions from given assumptions without recognizing the increasing irrelevance of the assumptions being used. Jacques Ellul described this pattern in *The Technological Society*. His conclusion was that man is unable to control the technology he has created, because he does not know how to change the fundamental-assumption pattern from which he works. Since Ellul wrote, the use of INTER has become still more pervasive because of the amount of time and effort that is being spent developing logical computer languages.

What happens, however, if we look at the opposite side of the issue? Once we cease to be mesmerized by the problems which stem from the wrong uses of INTER, we discover that there are also major possibilities in our growing understanding of INTER. However, to gain the possible advantages we must learn to employ INTER intelligently. If we *do* know our goals and the *real* conditions in which these goals must be achieved, INTER can be used to discover the logical steps which must be taken. INTER and computers make it possible to reduce significantly the time lag between the creation of a new goal and its effective implementation.

INTER and computers also provide the potential for organizing on the basis of process rather than on the basis of permanent projects. They help to make it possible to move out of structural-authority patterns into sapiential-authority patterns. For example, the university campus today organizes its intellectual activity on the basis of a catalog which is printed once a year. The university system is therefore necessarily inflexible and structured. Almost all courses run the same length of time and, more often than not, are scheduled to meet at the same time every week.

The present form of catalog was developed when the task

of compiling and printing a catalog on a continuing basis was infeasible, for it had to be carried out by human beings. The availability of INTER to program computers coupled with rapid printouts and visual-display mechanisms, makes it possible *continuously* to add new course offerings as well as to end those classes which cease to be relevant. The courses on campus could change as the interests of teachers and students evolved.

The major barrier to more flexible communication and organization at this point is not the lack of understanding of techniques and technology. We have the basic tools in INTER and computers. Rather, the barrier is that those who now hold structural-authority positions fear that the removal of their power to command would lead to inefficiency and idleness. The present catalog with fixed hours of meeting and fixed lengths for courses makes it possible for structural authority to be used to determine whether a set task is being completed. The more flexible the system, the less possibility there is of evaluating objectively the performance of those within it. As flexibility increases the only relevant criterion becomes subjective: the perception of the student himself as to his own progress and that of the teacher as to what has been learned.

A fully flexible situation seems inconceivable to many of those who now hold structural authority. Those who believe in sapiential authority claim that it would be far more effective than present systems if we would stop looking for problems and recognize the possibilities inherent within present situations. They argue that, while it was possible within the structural system for an administrator to determine whether the *letter* of the obligation was being fulfilled, there was no way to determine that the spirit of the educational process was understood or applied. They also argue that a change in the basic drives of human beings is taking place now that it is technologically feasible to feed, clothe, and shelter every human being. They argue that the whip and the carrot, which were used to motivate people in structural-authority systems, are no longer effective. Indeed, they go further and claim that positive and negative sanctions cannot be used as the basis for effective organization in today's world.

It is at this point that "old world" and "new world" people find their greatest difficulty in communication. Those who still accept the industrial-era view argue that men are inherently idle and lazy and that they will do nothing in the absence of external pressures. Those in the new world accept the idea that most human beings did indeed require external sanctions in the industrial era. They argue, however, that in today's conditions, when abundance is a free gift, people have become interested in their own self-actualization and are searching for activities where they can contribute most effectively.

New-world people concentrate on creating the institutions needed for the communications era rather than on converting those still thinking in industrial-era styles. They do this for two reasons. First, they wish to provide the possibility of meaningful activity to those who have already entered the communications era. Second, they know that it is unreasonable to expect anybody to choose to give up his existing patterns of behavior unless alternative patterns are shown to be feasible. The best way to encourage people to move out of the industrial era into the communication era is to show them new, attractive behavior patterns.

Those in the new world see the present disintegration of the society in a different way from those still living in the industrial era. Instead of arguing that our present crisis is caused by the loss of stabilizing factors, they see America's growing instability as the inevitable result of the industrial way of life. New-world thinkers argue that the basic crisis results from the fact that many individuals are looking for activity which will provide an opportunity for self-actualization, but they are unable to find it. They argue that the primary drive of the communication era is for self-actualization and that the frustration of this drive is causing our crisis. They believe that cop-outs into drugs, sex, and violence must be anticipated until man's primary drive can find meaningful expression.

The difference between excess and abundance

INTER is the major factor which has led to an increase in the amount that can be produced with a given amount of effort. The incapacity of America to absorb all that can be produced has led to policy patterns which hold down production and to a neo-Luddite revolt aiming to prevent the introduction of machines. But even these two forces have not been able to disguise completely the shift from scarcity to excess, from a society in which almost all people had too little to a society where much of the population is trying to find ways to integrate ecofact availability into a satisfactory life-style.

Uncontrolled INTER necessarily produces excess. Excess is a condition of "too much" while scarcity is a condition of "too little." If we are to move *beyond* excess into abundance, the unpleasant realities inherent in excess must become obvious to individuals and the society. We must perceive that both scarcity and excess are undesirable conditions: they both harm people and ecosystems.

It is only when this perception has been achieved that we shall be free to examine seriously the possibility of replacing scarcity-excess with a state of abundance. Abundance emerges as we move from structural authority to sapiential authority. Sapiential-authority systems require the further development of the competence of individuals beyond that necessary in the industrial era. Abundance only emerges when there is profound individual and societal self-discipline based on sapiential authority.

Abundance does not permit everybody to consume everything that he can conceivably want. Rather, abundance requires that each individual and society limit itself to those ecofacts which are truly necessary for self-development. Abundance, therefore, is not a "middle road" between two apparent extremes of scarcity and excess. We need a new model to discuss abundance. It will be found beyond our present dichotomizing, dualistic style of thinking. In effect, abundance lies on a different plane from that of scarcity-excess, and its implications *cannot* be understood by using industrial-era styles of thought.

The last paragraph clarifies the nature of the change between the scarcity-excess era and the abundance era. It also makes clear another aspect of sapiential authority. We have developed a culture in which we permit certain people— advertisers, public-relations experts, packagers, etc.—deliberately to increase the amount of ecofacts that the individual feels he needs. We have developed a society which can only function if those who try to sell ecofacts succeed in convincing the public that they need things which previously seemed unimportant.

If we are to enter the abundance era, we must eliminate this pattern. People must discover for themselves their requirements for their self-development and self-actualization. (The temptation here is to fall back into dichotomizing languages, to argue that people need to discover how to use as "little" as possible rather than as "much" as possible. Such quantitative measures are quite simply irrelevant.) The commercial apparatus necessary to increase sales in order to ensure economic balance in the industrial era must be dismantled. Once this has been accomplished, the problem/ possibility of determining what is needed falls on each individual, each family, and each community. It will therefore be critically important in the communications era that full and accurate information on ecofact quality and availability be known. Only computer-based information systems will be adequate for this task.

Moving out of the scarcity-excess dichotomy into abundance requires far more responsibility from each human being. The requirement that we move into sapiential-authority systems means that the human race must now grow up. The human race will only survive if it develops the qualities required to meet the new challenges which it has imposed on itself. Mankind's survival now depends on man's own wisdom.

An economic explanation

A parallel argument can be made in more directly economic terms. Economics has always defined itself as the science which endeavors to economize scarce resources. In the past, we argued that labor, land, and machinery were the scarce resources. We are still thinking and acting as if this were true. Today, however, it is more realistic to argue that the shortages are land, time, and creativity.

The inclusion of land in both lists is highly significant. Economists have largely lost sight of the reality so clearly proclaimed by Ricardo that the percentage of income going to landowners would necessarily increase over time because it is impossible to enlarge significantly the amount of available land. We are still assuming that we can treat the economic problems raised by an essentially static quantity of land in the same way as we can handle the economic problems raised by variable resources such as capital, machinery, and labor. As the ecology movement encourages an understanding of the differing status of land, this will inevitably increase the pressures which are already emerging against land speculation and misuse.

Because we have so far believed that labor and capital are the basic economic shortages, our economic measures are primarily calculated in these terms. The basic method of calculating productivity today is in terms of the number of man-hours it takes to produce a given amount of an ecofact. Such a calculation assumes that the factor which makes the primary difference to levels of productivity is the inputs made by labor.

If we take even a cursory glance at the real situation, we discover this means of calculation at best oversimplifies reality —and at worst totally distorts it. The amount of *effort* made by the average worker has declined since the nineteenth century. Today the output of *human* energy required to produce ecofacts is far lower than in the past.

The worker is able to produce more using less effort because he has access to machines. Economists who perceive this reality argue that we should not measure productivity in terms of manpower but rather in terms of units of capital. This proposal has not been widely adopted, partly because of the difficulties inherent in calculating the value of capital and partly because it too provides only a partial picture of the real causes of productivity increase.

In effect, the prime reason for rapid productivity increase is to be found in a factor which affects the performance of both men and machines. This factor is the amount of information available to men and incorporated in machines. Productivity increases are the result of the effective application of new information. In a sense, machines simply freeze information in the form known to the maker at the time that he produces the machine. The more the maker knows, the more production can be achieved from the machine using the same amount of raw materials and energy.

There are, therefore, very great potentials for increasing productivity in coming years. Western societies are rapidly increasing the amount of available information. In addition, there are now many attempts to cross-relate information: experience has shown that exchanges across existing fields of study can create synergies[1] of great importance.

Information and production

It is the potential for growth and interrelation of information which makes it possible for mankind to avoid its apparently probable destruction. For example, recycling resources makes it possible to do more with less. It may be helpful to list a few examples of the patterns which could be developed if we should really devote ourselves to recycling ecofacts presently considered as waste. Because the examples which follow are still in the development stage, they may well change before they can be applied. But the general directions appear valid.

---

[1] Synergies can be defined in this context as situations where the outputs from a given interaction are greater than the sum of the apparent inputs.

—One of the basic worldwide crises is water. The United States is one of the prime users. It employs, for example, approximately 3,805 gallons of water per capita per day for food production, as compared to 407 gallons per capita per day in India. However, the lavish utilization of water results from a lack of intelligent design. It is not a necessary condition. It has long been known that many ecofacts can be produced with a far less water use, but marketives have felt no real obligation to try to save water, both because it was cheap and because there was no real appreciation of the overall water picture.

The potentials for turning present wastes into productive resources is suggested by experience in an arid seacoast region of Mexico. The *Bulletin of Atomic Scientists* reports that University of Arizona scientists have created an integrated system that provides power, water, and food.

> Waste heat from engine-driven electrical generators is used to de-salt sea water. The resulting fresh water, in turn, is piped to vegetables planted within controlled-environment greenhouses of air-inflated plastic. . . . Moisture losses from arid-area field-crops, by evaporation and transpiration, are enormous. In a sealed-in environment, that moisture is trapped. . . . In addition to strawberries, 18 kinds of vegetables, grown in this manner, have been harvested directly from beach sand.

In effect, water can be saved in very large proportions if systems are rethought in terms of minimal water use rather than maximal immediate profit.

—A second worldwide crisis results from the rapidly growing volume of wastes. Part of the problem stems from the sheer volume of present wastes and part from our growing recognition that present methods of disposing of wastes are dissipating the resources required for the continuing survival of man. Once again, it is clear that a substantial part of the problem arises from the fact that we have paid little attention to its existence and have failed to adjust our socioeconomy to the critical importance of recycling. In many cases, companies and municipalities which do install environmentally desirable methods for recovering raw materials are still finding difficulty in disposing of the salvaged materials. It is "cheaper," for example, to make paper from felled trees than from recycled paper.

A report published by the United States Atomic Energy Commission suggests that this problem can be brought under control in the long run by using a fusion torch with ultra high temperature plasmas. A fusion torch can reduce *any* material to its basic elements.

> The use of the fusion torch is not only an alternative to pollution problems, but also has the potential, using energy from controlled nuclear fusion, for a closed-cycle economy which can solve the materials problems of the world by simply circulating a material from one form to another. . . . While not attempting to minimize the large amount of research both on fission and on fusion torch physics, it is entertaining to speculate on the vision this concept provides of the future—large cities, operated electrically by clean, safe fusion reactors that eliminate the city's waste products and generate the city's raw materials. . . . The vision is there, its attainment does not appear to be blocked by nature. Its achievement will depend on the will and the desire of men to see that it is brought about.

Many of those reading this volume may tend to dismiss this possibility on the grounds that it is not yet proved that we can achieve fusion power. However, we can no longer afford to ignore potential developments until they have been *proved* feasible. This is the pattern we have adopted up to the present time: the result has been the development of acute socioeconomic crises.

Others may reject many or all of the possibilities put forward here because they involve still further use of technology.

Such a rejection is based on a romantic fallacy—the belief that mankind still has the option to return to an earlier, simpler era. We have foreclosed that option. Those who wish can examine whether or not we were wise to force ourselves to rely so heavily on technology. But those who are interested in realistic policy requirements must accept the fact that mankind cannot now abandon technology.

—There is much concern about the consequences of the destruction of topsoil and the damage to land by strip-mining. Once again much of the damage was avoidable if only the priorities of individuals and the society had been different. If present trends continue, the consequences can, of course, be as grim as the negative scenario suggests, but there are possibilities as well.

For example, in a brochure put out by the National Coal Association, it is stated that ". . . in Illinois the apple trees on mined land produce more abundantly and resist disease more vigorously than their neighbors on adjoining unmined land." In Southern Illinois cows "feed on a pasture which was once a strip mine. Half the field was mined with a wheel excavator which left the field much as it was originally. The other half was mined with a shovel which mixed the strata of the earth. Evidently bringing layers of unused soil to the surface uncovers valuable nutrients, since the cows eat the grass from the shovel-mined area before hunger drives them to the other half of the pasture."

Examples of the hopeful trends arising from growing knowledge could be multiplied to fill a whole book. They can also be discovered by anybody who attempts to read, view, and listen in an attempt to discover our possibilities. It is critical, however, that we do not permit these possibilities to be perceived as new exponential trends. We must make sure that they become integrated into a systemic model.

The evidence that systemic thinking is being created

There are several types of people who are already moving out of linear patterns into systemic patterns. Indeed, there are already enough systemically-organized groups to make a profoundly significant difference. However, the movement toward systemic patterns must be clearly perceived before we can benefit fully from it. Such a recognition will have highly positive results. The theory of the Jesuit theologian Teilhard de Chardin that there is a rapid convergence in intelligent self-interest is today proving out in practice.

—Marketives are finding that the discovery of cross-relationships between existing knowledge is critical to their profitability. One increasingly common form of organization designed to achieve synergy is the task force which is brought together to solve a specific problem. Task forces are self-organizing. The model is well-known but its *fundamental* significance is only now being appreciated. There is, in fact, a curious anomaly in the situation of managements today. Management *theory* is largely systemic and sapiential. The *practice* of management, however, is still largely linear and structural. In addition, top management makes few efforts to ensure the extension of the systemic implications of management theory to the general society.

—Those people who are at the leading edges of their disciplines are finding that the linear patterns of existing knowledge are inadequate to express the truths they have discovered. All too often, indeed, any attempt to express systemic truths within the bounds of a discipline leads to the individual being expelled from the discipline. Systemic truth forces an individual to move beyond existing disciplines. A major synergy is now developing as a consequence. Those who have grown beyond various disciplines are discovering that they are able to communicate together—the physical scientist with the social scientist, the artist with the mathematician. We are rapidly reaching the point where a systemic theory could be developed and understood if the society were willing to support this process with the necessary resources.

—It is clear that many in the younger generation do not think linearly: television is probably partly responsible for this change. They have not, of course, learned to think in fully systemic terms as yet: if they had this book would be largely unnecessary. Today's younger generation is in transition. Only some of its members have crossed the divide from a world based on structural authority to a world based on sapiential authority. Many more of them are willing to make the effort to change if helped and encouraged to do so.

The consequences of systemic thinking

The potential for change today is explosive rather than incremental. We can no longer assume that change itself will be linear. Rather there will be burst patterns of change. The consequences of change in several areas will either be brought together by intellectual thinking or will fuse through world events: the consequences will be an order of magnitude greater than the events to which our thinking and our institutional patterns are geared.

The space program is the proof of the importance of systemic thinking. Whether or not one believes that reaching the moon was important, it is critical that we fully comprehend the scope of the breakthroughs which were essential in order for this goal to be achieved. Those who thought linearly at the beginning of the sixties were convinced that the moon could not be reached within the decade. It was the effective use of system thinking which made the feat possible.

There are other examples of successful system thinking. The coming Green Revolution promises to increase agricultural production to such an extent that we can avoid famine in most parts of the world. New strains of rice and other grains, coupled with an increased understanding of climate, has brought about very large potential increases in yields.

The Green Revolution, however, requires not only the planting of new strains of grains but also the rapid extension of the irrigated areas, the availability of large quantities of fertilizers and pesticides, and the potential for large-scale marketing. It will also cause a large-scale social revolution in the areas in which it develops.

A smaller but more pervasive example is the increased

systemic thinking in computer programming. Those who first programmed computers used linear rather than systemic thinking. However, the meshing of linear subprograms into overall software systems has tended to create a type of computer programming which can be called protosystemic. This protosystemic programming has led to rapid increases in efficiency. In addition, the need for programmers is declining as computers increasingly program themselves. In the future there will only be a place for programmers who fully understand the tasks they are performing.

The successes of systemic thinking naturally lead to a rapid demand for the further extension of systemic thinking. The following argument is increasingly heard in the United States. "If it is possible to reach the moon in a single decade, it should surely be possible to do a better job of solving our problems on earth." The system problems involved in solving man's problems are, of course, several orders of difficulty greater than those involved in reaching the moon. But this does not reduce the political significance of the demand.

In effect, systemic thinking is based on a different mathematics from linear thinking. Linear thinking is based on addition and subtraction. Systemic thinking is based on multiplication and division. This is the reason why the potential for change is so dramatically increased as one moves from linear thinking to systemic thinking.

The breakpoint for the human race

We *cannot* return to the linear, structural authority of the industrial era. We *must* develop the systemic, sapiential authority of the communications era. As systemic thinking is multiplicative rather than additive, we are therefore inevitably faced with rates of change that our present additive institutions were not designed to manage or control.

We are now able to state more clearly the reason why abundance is not possible within the scarcity-excess continuum. Abundance can only emerge when we create systemic, sapiential authority systems. Abundance develops when man becomes aware that resources are inherently limited but that his intelligent management of them can ensure the availability of sufficient possibilities for everybody to meet his real needs. A world of abundance requires that human beings and societies recognize their potentials and their limitations.

Abundance and waste cannot coexist. In an abundance society, recycling of resources is essentially complete. Abundance only becomes possible when we have internalized the insight that we live on Spaceship Earth with fixed resources, except for a massive continuing input of energy.

The effective functioning of an abundance society requires that individuals act to ensure the availability of the resources required if the society is to remain cohesive and healthy.

There is no doubt that our present energy resources, communication abilities, and transportation networks are adequate to produce a state of abundance in large parts of the world within a brief period of years if we were to commit ourselves to the task. The extent of our technological competence is now so great that there are few effective limits to our capabilities. The problem today is that we are still committed to using these capabilities for the production of excess rather than for moving into a condition of abundance. The danger we face in the immediate future is that the growth of this excess will choke off any chance of achieving abundance.

We must, however, face a basic reality. The points made in this chapter have been made many times before. While they may be slightly more persuasive because of the overall framework in which they have been placed, it would be naïve to assume that they communicate immediately and effectively the points which need to be made.

We now know a considerable amount about the ways learning takes place. In particular, we can show that true learning of new perceptions—as opposed to training in old ones—cannot normally be achieved linearly. The next chapter therefore serves to introduce—and justify—the fundamentally different style of presentation which follows it.

We have been driven back once more to the fundamental problem/possibility which makes the full perception of the ecological issue so difficult. As we make the transition from the industrial era to the communications era, we are not only concerned with a different set of priorities. We must, in addition, develop a totally new world view which involves new communication styles and new cultural patterns. *There is no way that these two processes can be disassociated from each other.* It was the attempt of the environment movement to change policies and priorities without changing communication styles and cultural patterns which has prevented true success.

CHAPTER 7   *THE LEARNING PROCESS*

Most present discussions of teaching and learning start from the assumption that we still have no hard information about the processes by which learning takes place or the consequences of various styles of learning. In actual fact, we do have considerable knowledge about these subjects at the present time, but we are slow to apply it. One of the reasons for this slowness is, of course, the general inertia of the society. The other reason is that the society has a very large investment, both human and financial, in present methods of thinking, and it is therefore unwilling to alter them if this can possibly be avoided.

Education and training

Understanding the process of learning requires the use of a critical distinction between education and training. Training is the process of conveying to people the information which is already known about a particular topic as rapidly as possible. Education enables people to examine the situation in which they find themselves and to create behavior patterns suitable to deal with that situation.

Let us take up the issues involved in training first. The goal of training is to ensure that the individual comprehends the

already known as fully and rapidly as possible. Training per-
petuates existing patterns of understanding and therefore
reinforces existing trends. In a stable society, most of what
the individual needs to know can be made available using
training techniques. It can be assumed that what is known
by the society in which he lives is valid and will remain valid.

During the last decade there have been highly significant
developments in our knowledge of how to train individuals.
We are learning how an individual can absorb known information more efficiently. The success of the input process is
typically measured by the ability of the individual to repeat
the material on demand and without change.

The family of techniques known as programmed learning
fall into the training category. Material is set out so that the
individual can go back over material that he does not understand as many times as is necessary, while moving ahead as
rapidly as his speed of comprehension makes possible. Effective programmed learning, coupled with prospects of chemical
enhancement of learning capacity, promise to make it possible to train people in all areas with great speed.

Training starts from the proved fact that information is
most rapidly absorbed when presented in small pieces. People
are provided with a sense of achievement as each piece of
information is learned. The use of training techniques therefore *necessarily* prevents an individual from discovering
whether the overall pattern of information he is receiving
makes sense.

Training techniques are, of course, appropriate for many
of the tasks which the individual must learn to do. It would
be impossibly time-consuming for every person to understand
fully the total rationale behind everything that he does.
Everybody must expect to be trained in certain areas. There
are conventional patterns which must be accepted. For example, it is sufficient to train most automobile drivers. We are,
indeed, in urgent need of more effective training techniques
which can be used on all appropriate occasions to limit the
repetitive drudgery involved in training.

But training is clearly not always suitable. The speed of change is now so great that many of the cultural and societal responses we have learned in the past are unsuitable to the future we are entering. If we limit ourselves to training students in the old patterns, not only do we deprive them of the possibility of learning for themselves how to improve their own patterns of behavior, but we limit the chances that the total society will be able to adapt with sufficient speed to the requirements of tomorrow.

Training can be described as learning from the outside. Through training one acquires a particular skill to do a particular task well, but one has no real knowledge of *why* one is being efficient.

On the other hand, the individual who is educated is not only aware of the most effective behavior patterns in his society, but he also understands *why* they are the most effective behavior patterns. If conditions change, he therefore has the knowledge to create new behavior patterns suitable to the new conditions easily and effectively.

A science-fiction story dramatizes the distinction between education and training. The story was about a society in the far future which had learned to train by direct input of information to the brain. In this imagined world, the vast majority of the society was instantaneously trained to do a particular job. The skills were implanted in them. The few people in the culture who had special conceptual abilities were educated so that they could continue to improve the patterns of training available to the rest of the society.

This science-fiction story is valuable because it does clarify when training is effective and when education is required. It is also useful because the story so clearly betrays one of the unconscious biases of present Western cultures: it is based on the belief that an elite can rule the society and that everybody else can be freed from the need to make real decisions. In a dynamic world, every individual needs the ability to relate changing conditions in the outside world to his own particular role. The individual who has only been trained is therefore doomed to an increasingly unsatisfactory life. The educated individual, on the other hand, can alter his life-style to accord with changing realities and can thus continue to fulfill his purposes.

One of the more interesting consequences of the distinction between education and training is that the subjects in which an individual should be trained and those in which he should be educated necessarily vary with the *subjectively* defined purposes of the individual. The communications engineer needs to be educated in the design of the computer and trained in the foreign languages which he needs to know if he is to be an effective communications engineer. The individual who wishes to be creative in foreign languages needs to be educated in those languages but may also need to be trained how to use the computer so that he can employ it in his foreign-language work.

It is therefore necessary for us to learn that one pattern of education is not more valuable than another. The agriculturalist is as necessary for the good life as the economist. Those knowledgeable in child care are as necessary as the philosopher. In the diverse world of tomorrow, we shall recognize that we are all mutually interdependent and that our present concept of a necessary hierarchy of roles is a hangover from the structural-authority thinking of the industrial era.

The meaning of education

One helpful definition of education is "the process of helping a person to discover how he can best live in the world in which he finds himself." Given the present necessity for fundamental change, it is clear that one of the main tasks of education today is to discover new personal and societal interconnections rather than to inform people about those which existed in the past. In effect, we must cease to analyze in terms of past categories, and we must learn to think in new ways which are relevant in the present and will be critical to understanding the future.

Education occurs when people learn to seek the new, relevant questions rather than aim further to refine existing answers. An individual is educated when he has learned to look at data in such a way that the questions inherent in the material spring to his mind. In other words, education occurs when the individual learns to question the assumptions which lie behind existing classifications of information rather than to study the information which is conveyed by the present classifications.

John Cage, the artist, has stated that " measurements measure measuring means." This suggests that it is the patterns of the culture which determine what is considered worth measuring—and, by extension, observing. These basic cultural patterns are far more critical for achieving understanding of the nature of the culture than are the precise levels reached by the various indicators. Western societies measure economic indicators and still largely ignore social indicators. We are therefore justified in concluding that Western societies care profoundly about their economic health but pay little attention to social health. At a deeper level, Western societies pay attention to anything quantitatively measurable and ignore those realities which can only be expressed in qualitative terms.

The current discontent on campus can best be understood in terms of a demand that education should replace training. The difficulties in such a change are immense. Present-day teachers and their tools were developed to promote efficient training. Most existing teachers are only comfortable when they have the certainty which comes from providing answers. They are profoundly threatened when they engage in a joint search for new questions. In effect, they want to keep their structural authority. However, education is only possible on the basis of sapiential authority.

This topic needs further discussion. Before continuing, however, we must learn how the brain holds information and how new information can be effectively introduced.

Fundamental learning theory

Education, defined as it is above, necessarily requires change in existing ideas as well as the addition of ideas. Education of course necessarily takes place within the context of an existing set of ideas and concepts. Thus old ideas must always be displaced by new ideas if education is to occur.

The degree to which education is possible depends on the complexity of the organism. The wider the repertoire of responses possible to the organism, the more probable it is that true education can take place. Until quite recently, there was a tendency to assume that only man was capable of true education—that is, learning new response patterns. There was an attempt to place a clear-cut barrier between man and all other species.

This simplistic belief is now recognized as untrue. A simpler organism, of course, relies more completely on hard programming than man does; its autonomic nervous system is therefore more important than its voluntary nervous system. Nevertheless, many organisms besides man have within them the capacity for extensive learned behavior.

The extent of learnable behavior is obvious in circuses and aquaria. Such behavior is often dismissed on the grounds that it is taught by human beings. However, this belief is not fully accurate. For example, a dolphin created for an individual with whom he worked a wide range of behavior patterns, some of which had never been observed in dolphins before. The dolphin could not have been taught by the human being. Rather the dolphin initiated new response patterns.

In addition, there are many confirmed cases where animals and birds have learned for themselves how to adapt to man-made change in conditions. For example, jays in England learned to peck the aluminum caps off milk bottles in order to drink from them.

The first step in understanding brain patternings is to

recognize that there is no single, objective reality. A cat, a dog, a flea, a frog, an American, a Chinese, a farmer, a businessman placed in the same environment will perceive sharply different parts of the total "reality." A goal of perceiving the totality of reality is neither desirable nor feasible. If we did perceive everything that exists in a given situation, we should be so overwhelmed that we would be unable to act in any way.

(Many people will need to stop at this point in order to recognize how differently they do perceive compared to people from other generations and other cultures, let alone compared to other organisms.)

In effect, we must always screen reality to discover those parts of the pattern which are relevant to us. Some of the screens which determine our range of perception are genetic. These screens are hard programmed. They determine the sounds, colors, sizes we can perceive without the use of instruments: for example, a dog can hear a whistle inaudible to the human ear. These genetic screens create limits which it is difficult and sometimes impossible to change, although man has, of course, developed many instruments which expand the normal reach of his senses.

We also use other screens which are based on the cultural patterns of the society. It is possible to explain events in many ways. For example, categories of understanding can be based on magic and supernatural beings or in terms of scientific rationality.

We can clarify this concept by perceiving that, until recently, each culture and subculture had its own set of screens. Each culture found the reality created by its set of screens fully valid. Strangers, however, found the images of reality used in the culture strange and often bizarre. In effect, mankind lived in a world in which there was a large hall full of distorting mirrors. Each culture drew its reality from what it perceived in one of the distorting mirrors. Each culture believed that its own perception was uniquely valid while all others were incorrect, laughable, and possibly dangerous.

A continuing problem must be emphasized at this point. There has always been a strong tendency in the United States to assume not only that the vision of reality achieved by Americans was valid but that it was the only possible way to see the world. The whole tenor of this book challenges this view. We can now see that the linear, structural patternings which are predominant in America represent a highly limited view of the world.

In effect, Americans need to recognize that there are many sets of screens for viewing reality. Thus each person will have a *unique* overall viewpoint. This does not mean, however, that agreement cannot be reached between people when they jointly confront the same situation. Experience shows that it is the people who are most aware of the uniqueness of their screening processes who can most rapidly agree on the steps required within a specific situation.

Once we understand the reality of the screening process, we can learn how it determines our actions. We see part of reality. Our inability to perceive the total reality means that our view is inherently somewhat distorted. We can, however, only act on the basis of the view of reality which we have, for this is the only view available to us. Definitionally, the remainder of reality has been screened out. It therefore follows that, if an individual changes the way he perceives reality, he *necessarily* alters his action patterns.

How people change their reality screens is the subject of the remainder of this chapter. The difficulties involved in shifting screens are far larger than may appear at first sight. An individual's screening pattern is an intricately connected net, and a shift in one part of the net therefore involves complex, interrelated shifts in many other areas.

We now know that the brain can be described in terms of a fantastically complex set of interrelated conditioned responses. If an individual's screening process lets in a particular pattern of reality over an extended period of time, the brain will set up a response pattern to control consequent actions which is quasi-automatic. Such a response pattern is called a conditioned response. Repetition of the response pattern reinforces it so that the response becomes less selectively controllable.

Some of these conditioned responses are hard programmed through genetic history and are therefore difficult, if not impossible, to change within a single generation. But many conditioned responses are learned from the society or on one's own. It is these learned responses which can be changed when a person is confronted with situations for which his responses are inadequate.

It is normally assumed that the appropriate method of changing a person's view of the world is to argue with him directly, to challenge the view he holds. In reality, such a technique is almost necessarily ineffective. This is because the view which is held is logical to the individual holding the view. That is, it fits his understanding of the situation and his own world view. (The validity of this statement extends to the thought patterns of many of the insane: in effect, we call people insane when their thought patterns diverge strongly from those of the culture.)

Direct contradiction of views results, therefore, in the ballet debate. Each side makes its own cogent argument, but they do not alter each other's view. Indeed, the net effect is to reinforce existing views, because the conditioned responses have been reactivated and have therefore been strengthened.

It appears to be impossible to overcome directly an established conditioned response. On the other hand, a conditioned response will decay as it becomes less useful to the individual. This means, in effect, that the individual must discover *other* responses which are more relevant or adequate to the situation in which he finds himself. Conditioned responses decay as new, more attractive responses arise to replace them.

It seems that the effective way to alter conditioned responses is to enable an individual to perceive the importance of issues which he had previously not discovered. If this is carefully done, the individual will enlarge his pattern of thinking and will eventually find it necessary to reconsider his existing conditioned responses in the light of his increased knowledge.

The reality that one cannot directly destroy individual conditioned responses is paralleled in the social sphere. Questions which seem critical at one period of history are not solved but bypassed. The Middle Ages wanted to discover how many angels could dance on the head of a pin. We do not care. Similarly, as we move into the communications era, we shall leave behind many of the issues which were considered critical during the industrial era.

We must, however, clearly face the reality that, at this point in time, people have been brought up within sharply different cultural patterns and that they will not perceive identical realities or act in the same way in the same situation. It is for this reason that an individual who was born in the nineteenth century sees the world differently from an individual who was born between the two world wars and that they will both perceive the world differently as compared with the individual born after the explosion of the atomic bomb.

Today, cultures are splintering into subcultures and subsubcultures with extreme rapidity. The screens used by groups and individuals are fragmenting rapidly, and their views of reality are becoming so disparate that the possibility of communication is vanishing. Communication is not possible without the existence of a minimal common reality frame. The survival of man now depends on people with differing world views learning to perceive each other's screening processes and then working to create new patterns of thought which include the necessary key elements of the communications era. This can only be done within an abundance condition.

Change in conditioned responses

Let us now look at the specific patterns which emerge as people argue. For example, there is today an increasingly acute divergence between the producers of electric power, who perceive the need for the rapid creation of more electrical capacity in order to prevent the breakdown of the electrical grid, and the environmentalists, who fear the polluting consequences of massive increases in the production of electrical power.

We presently expect this disagreement to be argued angrily and, increasingly, violently. When there is no agreement, society accepts the fact that the disagreeing groups should bring as much pressure on each other as they can. It is apparently believed that the truth will emerge from confrontations of ideas and also from confrontations in boardrooms, on picket lines etc.

Once we translate this conventional widsom into what we know about conditioned responses, we discover its essential fallacy. Conditioned responses in the brain are like all other forms of activity pattern. If they are used, they are strengthened. If on the other hand they are not employed, they tend to atrophy. Arguments and confrontations of all types simply lead to reinforcement of currently held beliefs rather than to modifications in thinking.

In effect, the two sides in the electricity debate are putting forward two aspects of the overall argument: they are not actually disagreeing with each other. It is obviously correct to state that so long as America demands more electrical power, failure to generate this required power will lead to disastrous shutdowns in the electrical-power system and that shutdowns will damage the interests of the United States. It is also true, however, that continuation of the present increase in the demand for power in the United States—and the rest of the world—will necessarily lead to catastrophe unless there are profound changes in methods of power generation.

Any discussion about future policies must include three aspects. First, we must consider where we are presently moving and what will occur unless we make deliberate attempts to change this direction. Second, we must discover what we would wish the future to be like, including in our discussions the existing constraints on our direction of movement and the degree to which they can be changed. Third, we must see what policies we can devise to change from our present direction into the directions which seem desirable.

It is clear that the range of variables which we must consider is far wider than ever before, because of man's increased power. We can alter the genetic inheritance of man: we must therefore discover which of the possible changes will be favorable and which dangerous. We can modify the pattern of earth's weather: we must therefore discover which of the possible changes will be favorable and which dangerous. We can alter the nature of other organisms with which man interacts: we must therefore discover which of the possible changes will be favorable and which dangerous. And we must do all this in the context of brains which contain both biological limits and culturally conditioned responses which make it difficult to perceive clearly the "reality" we presently confront.

The process of education

How are we to help people discover for themselves the new conditioned responses which will permit them to act effectively within the new realities? It is this question which lies behind this chapter and, indeed, must inform all attempts to permit people to live in the future rather than in the past. Fortunately, we now have some clear concepts about the steps which are required. There are three steps which must be taken if there is to be real learning, real change in action patterns and thus the creation of new conditioned responses. They are first the provision of new, credible information, second, the availability of effective opportunities to discuss the information which has been received to discover the extent to which it is valid, third, the opportunity to act on the insights discovered and thereby create feedback patterns which will provide new, credible information.

(A) THE PROVISION OF CREDIBLE INFORMATION. Credibility is, of course, a subjective criterion. A member of the John Birch Society finds the information provided by his leaders credible. Similarly, a member of the Black Muslims finds the information provided by *his* leaders credible. However, if a Black Muslim leader were to speak to an audience of John Birchers, his information would not be credible. Nor would a John Bircher be credible in front of an audience of Black Muslims.

The examples given have deliberately been extreme in order to demonstrate the point. Unfortunately, the fragmentation of the national and world society is now proceeding so rapidly that few people are credible to more than a minute part of the population. This can be clearly seen in the fact that the media, which until recently were viewed as a method of obtaining unbiased information, are increasingly vilified on the grounds that they deliberately distort information.

In many ways our situation can only be compared to a modern Tower of Babel. Everybody is talking, and nobody is listening. Even when people are willing to listen, the language that each subgroup uses is so divergent that even if the *same* statement is being made by two groups, the essential similarities are not recognized. Many people and groups today are saying similar things but often fail to perceive this fact.

A striking example of this reality is the continuing fragmentation of the conservative movement in America, and indeed the world, at this point in time. A large number of groups are proclaiming that our only remaining hope is to find ways for the individual to have the opportunity to make decisions for himself. They also argue that large bureaucratic organizations are nonfunctional in present circumstances. This point is being made by much of the old right, by the new left, by the religious revival, and by many middle Americans who have no particular ideology or political affiliation. Unfortunately, however, the rhetorics used by the various conservative groups are so far apart that they do not perceive that they have anything in common. As a result, they cannot learn from each other, for their statements are mutually incredible.

The real conflict between philosophies in the United States is *not* along the lines presently discussed. The real issue is not in terms of the young fighting the old, the ravagers of the culture against its defenders, the Liberals against the Conservatives. Rather, the fundamental disagreement is between those who support structural authority and those who believe structural authority is unworkable. The real battle is between those who believe in the continuation of industrial-era systems and those who know that these systems are no longer effective.

Many of those who believe that they are supporting the industrial era are actually pulling down on themselves. One of the most startling examples of this reality is Vice-President Spiro Agnew. His attacks on the structural authority of the media are one of the primary factors ensuring that structural-authority systems will become effectively nonviable in the near future.

The minimum requirement for communication is, of course, credibility—not complete accuracy. Nobody has all the truth, and therefore nobody can provide answers to all the questions which can be raised. All that is required for the satisfactory accomplishment of the first step in the process of learning is that one is prepared to accept the fact that the person bringing information is not trying to manipulate it for his own purposes.

Most disagreements today do not involve one party being right and the other wrong. Rather, both parties are right, given the models of reality they are using. Credibility in this context can be defined as the belief that the person bringing information has pieces of the truth which deserve to be considered seriously. A speaker who does not meet these criteria will certainly do no good and may actually worsen the situation. For example, if a group of Black Muslims should listen to a John Bircher, it would certainly increase their intransigence: the same pattern would occur if a group of John Birchers should listen to a Black Muslim.

(B) THE AVAILABILITY OF EFFECTIVE OPPORTUNITIES TO DISCUSS THE INFORMATION WHICH HAS BEEN RECEIVED. Let us now assume that a group has listened to a speaker. If he has been seen as credible and not been ignored or dismissed out of hand, the group will have received new information. (We are excluding from consideration the all too common case where the speaker comes to tell the audience what they already know in the form which is most palatable to them.) This new information now needs to be examined by the individual to discover if it is sufficiently valid and relevant to be permanently incorporated into the brain, there to become part of new conditioned responses.

There are a few people whose listening and absorption skills are already so great that they can accomplish this task of examination by themselves. Most people, however, find it easiest to examine new ideas in group situations. Indeed, group discussion is essential to change if those addressed represent a continuing organization which already has operating rules and principles. Modification in the way the organization presently thinks and operates can only be made if all those involved become aware of the issues raised by modification.

It is usually very difficult to achieve effective change in the thought patterns of an ongoing organization. The difficulties involved are greatly increased by the fact that those within the organization often have a profoundly negative view of the attitudes of others in the organization. For example, one of the present key arguments in social work is whether one can trust an individual to act responsibly for himself or whether there must be constant bureaucratic supervision. In a typical social-work audience, a very large proportion of those present are prepared to trust those they are trying to help. However, they believe that their colleagues are not willing to act in the same way. Patterns of discussion are therefore usually ineffective, because most of the time is spent trying to convince others of the necessity of giving clients more freedom rather than recognizing that the problem is not in the attitudes of the group but in the political and organizational constraints affecting all those in the social-work profession.

To break out of these pessimistic biases, profoundly different structures must be created as compared to those generally used to cause discussion. Groups are normally formed to provide answers to already posed questions. When this is the intention, the group should use INTER to discover the one best way to solve the question which has been placed before it.

Alterations in conditioned responses cannot, however, occur in this way. People who have received new information must struggle to discover whether it is valid for them. They are not seeking answers to already posed questions. Rather, they must discover what the real questions are.

In effect, we have been engaging in this process throughout this book. We have been trying to demonstrate that the way we presently ask questions is inadequate and that we need to search for the appropriate questions. In effect, we need a different communication style.

When young and old discuss together, conversation often breaks down because the communication styles of the two age groups tend to be incompatible. Let us suppose that the subject of a discussion between these two age groups is "poverty." Older people are usually willing to assume that they know what is really meant by "poverty" and also that the abolition of poverty is desirable. This viewpoint is not acceptable to many of the young, to whom the word "poverty" has favorable as well as unfavorable connotations. Many of the young believe that an excess of material goods gets in the way of a satisfactory life.

In this case, the young and old fail to talk together because they fail to recognize the differences in their communication styles. The older group typically see themselves as having a clear agenda. They define their task as discovering how to abolish the problem of poverty. The younger group typically believes that the first necessity is to discover the real meaning of the agenda.

We have now discovered a further reason for our present Tower of Babel situation. Not only do people deny the credibility of others and use different words for similar things, they also have profoundly different ideas about the proper way to discuss questions.

What do we know about communication styles which permit the clearer definition of questions? Because nobody in the group can be expected to have all the necessary knowledge, we must expect that the conversation will often be nondirected and nondirective. The communication style required has been called OUTER and has been defined as "a blabbermouth language written on psychic tissue paper."

In order to discover needed new questions, people have to be prepared to raise points which they do not yet fully understand themselves but which they believe may be helpful in the movement toward comprehension. OUTER makes possible the building of the partial insights of various people into a larger insight which was not available to anybody in the group at the beginning of the discussion. OUTER permits a synergy process where one plus one equals more than two.

Unfortunately, the OUTER process can be easily blocked. Definitionally, OUTER conversation consists of partial insights. If anybody in the room insists that an individual complete a partial insight by saying, for example, "That's very interesting, can you tell me more," the person addressed will be unable to respond. This trick is often used by older people who are uncomfortable with OUTER. Because those talking OUTER become tongue-tied when asked such questions, the questioner feels justified in attacking the validity of the whole process.

OUTER, therefore, cannot be effective without a substantial level of trust. This is the reason why the words "psychic tissue paper" appear in the definition above. OUTER always involves discussion of assumptions, for it is one's assumptions which determine the questions which appear relevant. Discussion of one's assumptions necessarily provides information about the way one thinks, believes, and acts. People are naturally unwilling to share information of this type so long as they do not trust the other people in the room, for they fear that the information will be used against them.

It may be useful to compare and contrast OUTER with two other concepts. First, there is a close relationship between OUTER and dialogue. Unfortunately, the word "dialogue" has been used on all too many occasions to describe situations where people talk until they agree with the proposals which had been put before them by those with structural authority. OUTER, on the other hand, necessarily involves the elimination of all structural authority.

OUTER may also appear to some as being similar to sensitivity training. Actually, it is totally contradictory to most sensitivity sessions. Sensitivity training usually requires that one examine one's own emotions, explore them with others, and be prepared to justify them. In effect, sensitivity training is an advanced form of navel gazing. OUTER, on the contrary, requires the examination of the relationships and processes of the real world. The use of OUTER increases one's emotions and leads to self-perception and self-actualization. The two processes are not only different conceptually. Experience suggests that sensitivity training prevents the development of effective OUTER.

Successful OUTER provides the individual and the group with new insights. Under normal circumstances, they will be closer to reality than those with which the group started. But it would be utopian to assume that they will be complete or fully accurate. Only the test of experience can show to what extent the new insights are valid. One of the profound realities of the sapiential-authority system is that one always knows better tomorrow how to do what one did yesterday— *but only because one did it yesterday.*

(c) THE CREATION OF ACTION PATTERNS AND THE
EVALUATION OF FEEDBACK. One of the effects of successful
OUTER will be to make people more aware of the requirements
of the system in which they are living and to convince them
that they should be involved in improving this situation.

They will therefore be driven toward action. But the OUTER
insights they have achieved will not be *directly* translatable
into action patterns. Every real situation is constrained by its
past history. If it is decided that there is an urgent need to
change the educational system, one must then consider what
is the most effective way to do this. For example, one must
ask whether action should be on a national or a local scale.
In each case, what are the leverage points for change?

This third step into action requires another communication
style which has been called SITUATIONAL. If it has been
decided to alter the education system, the individual or group
concerned with change must understand the existing assumption patterns used by the educational profession and the
situations they are confronting sufficiently well that he can act
directly with them without confronting the Tower of Babel
problem. Effective change requires that those trying to achieve
it can work directly with those presently involved. The ability
to communicate effectively in SITUATIONAL is essential.

Failures to respect this requirement are commonplace. For
example, let us assume that some people become aware of
a genuine crisis which requires immediate action. All too
often, they assume that goodwill is enough, that they will be
effective if they announce their desire to be helpful. The com-
plaint of would-be change agents that they have been ignored
by the establishment can only too frequently be explained
in terms of their unwillingness to learn how to communicate
effectively on the subjects which concern them.

(This does not mean, of course, that the establishment is
without blame. At this point, those with structural authority
should be trying to find the people who have sapiential
authority. Ideally, much of the burden of translating new

ideas so they can be clearly perceived should be handled by those who presently have structural authority.)

How should an individual or a group decide where and on what level they wish to operate as change agents? A simple rule of thumb is that they should do what they can already do effectively plus 10 percent to permit them to enlarge their skills. A group or individual can be most effective when they use their existing skills. This should not cause any concern that one might end up stuck in a rut. If the individual does operate in those areas in which he is most competent and if he does take risks which are of a magnitude he can handle, he will find that he continuously grows and is drawn into new areas.

If people are to act effectively, they must be helped to find action possibilities at their own level of competence. We should not force a person who is interested in eliminating poverty to work in the ghetto unless he feels competent to do so. Well-meaning but blundering individuals and groups do more harm than good. It is, in fact, highly immoral to try to act in situations which one does not have the skills to handle. The patterns which result from unintelligent action may be highly destructive. The dangers are particularly great at the present time when very high levels of tension exist.

Successful action leads to results. Careful evaluation of the consequent feedback provides a new input of credible information which permits further learning. The circle is thus closed, and education becomes a continuing process.

The failure of education

We can now define what is needed for an effective education, and we can perceive why we are failing so completely. Education requires the input of credible information, the opportunity to discuss this information with people one trusts, and the possibility of putting one's new understandings into practice. The present education system fails in all three areas.

Some still believe that the information received by those

being educated is credible. This is true in a few limited areas. But it is absolutely incorrect in those areas which are most important for our survival—the social sciences. Our social sciences are based on sets of assumptions which had dubious validity in the late nineteenth and early twentieth centuries when most of them were created and which have no validity today. The information conveyed to students in these fields seems incredible to them. And they are right.

Information received by the student in the classroom is directly contradicted as he watches television and reads print media. This applies as much to entertainment programs as it does to the news. In addition, the assumptions of the social sciences are shown to be irrelevant by the life an increasing number of students are forced to adopt.

Students are still not normally given opportunities to discuss the information they are fed in the classroom. They are usually forced by the structures of school and university to accept the information they receive as correct, to ingurgitate it as completely and as accurately as possible, and then to regurgitate it.

Students are not expected—or normally permitted—to apply the knowledge they learn until they leave the school or university. Even when they do act, they are expected to respond to secondary rather than primary feedback. For example, student teachers are expected to respond to the reaction of the already trained teacher rather than to the direct feedback from the students whom they teach. Those students who have argued that they should be permitted to interact within the community are entirely correct in terms of educational theory. But their demand is unacceptable to professors and administrators.

The reasons are obvious. Professors and administrators were taught INTER as their primary communication style. The strictly logical communication style of INTER aims to discover the best way to carry through a task which has already been fully defined. INTER cannot be used at the same time as OUTER and SITUATIONAL. Any move away from the INTER training techniques now employed in schools and universities toward education using OUTER and SITUATIONAL communication styles would necessarily lead to many teachers becoming "students." It is not surprising, therefore, that most professors and administrators reject the profound educational reforms which are so urgently necessary.

What this book is trying to do

Books are normally written in INTER. This volume tries to break out of the INTER style. There are, however, strict limits on what we can achieve without your cooperation. Unless you choose to educate yourself, rather than train yourself, what we do will make little difference.

For example, a book cannot bring you the wide range of sensory experience you need to consider the real issues which we confront. What is valuable in the environment? Does true wilderness heal? If so, how do we preserve it? Does man need to be in touch with nature because of his past or can (should) we grow beyond it? The assumption patterns we bring to the study of ecology and the environment are necessarily based on our beliefs about such fundamental questions.

Nor can a book set up the discussion patterns which you will probably need if you are to consider successfully the validity of the ideas expressed in this volume. If you just read through the book, it will have minimal impact in teaching you new conditioned responses. If you are to learn new conditioned responses, you must make the effort to discover those who share your concern with the future.

There is one final point which we must make before we leave this chapter. Because of what we are trying to do, we have been using some systemic OUTER patterns throughout this book. As all of us are primarily used to linear INTER patterns, this will inevitably have been irritating to some readers. Now that you are more fully aware of the reasons for the break from linear patterns, it may be easier for you to control your irritation and to perceive the necessity for OUTER patterns.

There is one specific aspect of the OUTER style which should be mentioned at this point. It has proved necessary to employ a large amount of redundancy in this volume. The same point has been made in several different ways. The basic object has been to move the reader from acceptance of structural authority to an understanding of the need for sapiential authority if man is to survive. There is no single, neat way to make this point. Different people find it easiest to learn it in different ways.

The following chapter tries to provide further clues to the process involved in changing from perceiving the world as a mechanism to seeing it as a highly complex system whose survival depends on effective feedback.

We have used various techniques to suggest aspects of the issues with which we must deal. Some people will find all of the next chapter helpful. We hope that nobody will find it valueless. But we know that because each person is different, it is naïve to assume that everybody will learn from everything in the next chapter. Please skip those portions which are not helpful.

CHAPTER 8   ABUNDANCE IS A FREE GIFT

Yet he commanded the skies above,
he opened the doors of heaven
he rained down manna to feed them,
he gave them the wheat of heaven
                    Psalm 78:23–24

Abundance exists when the needs of human beings and other living organisms can be met from the resources available in the environment . . . . . .

SCARCITY IS DESTRUCTIVE

EXCESS IS DESTRUCTIVE

SCARCITY IS DESTRUCTIVE

C. and J. Thums

EXCESS IS DESTRUCTIVE

Atomic Energy Commission

C. and J. Thums

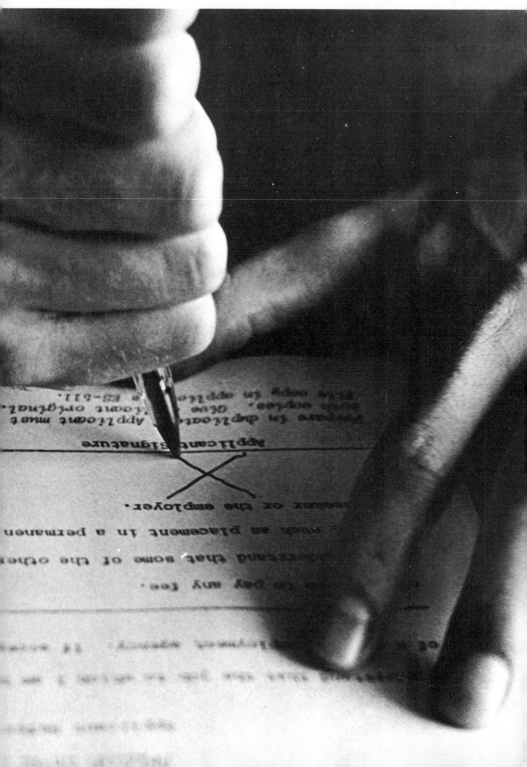

EXCESS IS DESTRUCTIVE

Wide World Photos

United Press International Photo

EXCESS IS DEHUMANIZING

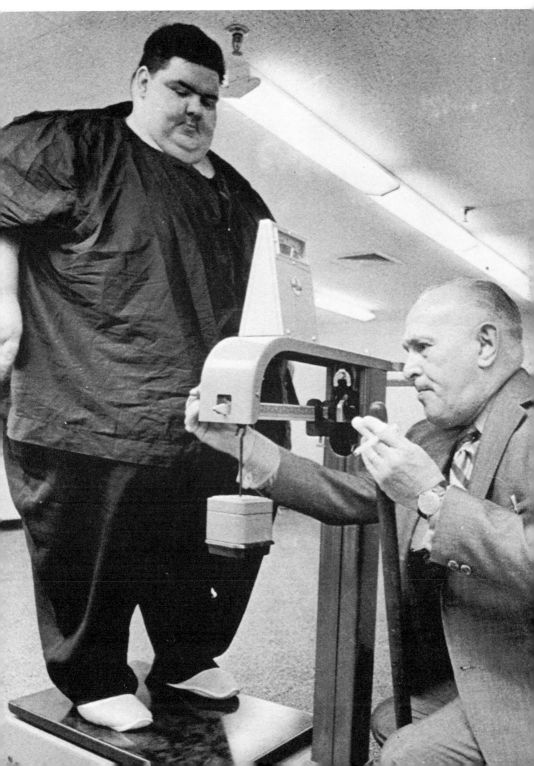

It was one of the most beautiful accounts in the history of advertising. We were selling sewing machines to Indians who couldn't run them because they had no place to plug them in. . . . We ran ads, we ran commercials, and we made a lot of bread. If you got the Indian to make the down payment, you were breaking even. The rest of the stuff was gravy.

—Jerry Della Femina,
From Those Wonderful Folks Who
Gave You Pearl Harbor

THE PROMISE OF AMERICA

The future of America is as limitless as the human spirit and the boundaries of space. But that future can only be realized with continuing courage and confidence plus a measure of self-discipline, for these are the qualities that have built America.

If you're uncertain about what lies ahead, remember this: the flow of products from American factories has more than doubled every twenty years in the past, but in the coming decade **alone** production of goods and services will more than double—to an unbelievable two trillion dollars! The impetus for this powerful growth is provided by research—itself one of our fastest growing industries. Research spending has soared from less than eleven billion dollars in 1958 to an estimated 25 billion dollars in 1969.

The prospect of the 1970's is enough to inspire
the most pessimistic. Among the problems
scheduled for wholesale attack in the 70's are
the cities, poverty and hunger, crime, water and
air pollution, and transportation.

The decade just ahead will see a U.S. labor force
swelled by 15 million, to a total of 99 million—
with a total population of nearly 240 million. The
largest increase will be in the group of Americans
between the ages of 25 and 34, the prime ages
for the formation of new families. There will be
10.3 million more "primary" families—mostly
young couples—for a total of 61.5 million. In fact,
in the year 1975 analysts predict that 2.5 million
marriages will take place.

This change in the age of population, plus their
steadily rising affluence, will bring an unheard-of
boom in housing, autos, appliances, furniture,
air conditioning and a broad variety of the things
young families want.

. . . The market for American goods and services
is only bounded by the limits of our imagination
and ingenuity.

. . . The opportunities are genuine and as vast
as our land. If we are to achieve their fulfillment,
all of us must contribute to the limits of our
abilities to meet the challenge we face.

. . . If we plan together, work together, we can
realize The Promise of America, for again the
time has come for great achievement.

a statement published by
Putnam Fund Distributors, Inc.,
Boston, Massachusetts

There is enough Chantilly in this bottle to shake her world.

Introducing nonviolent shaving.

An oil for the car that has everything.

Escape Your World. Embrace Ours.

Clairol brings you happiness.

You can become famous for your cocktails if you can lie with conviction.

Air condition your marriage.

Lead women around by the nose.

Give it to him. Drop by drop.

Coty originates the makeup that lets you go as far as you want.

The Walleys are polyunsaturating on their tailgate.

Cigarettes are like women: the best ones are thin and rich.

You could be Dodge material.

"Advertisers must think that women are stupid if they are to believe that a toothpaste will bring sex appeal."

Announcing: the almost real thing.

You lay that baby right down on the peg and nail it.

"People don't speak candidly on public issues. If they did, they wouldn't be trusted." Daniel Patrick Moynihan

Progress is our most important product.

It does what dropping a handkerchief used to do.

"Some advertisers act like women have brain damage."

We care how you live.

Men. Take it off, take it all off.

If you have any doubts about yourself, try something else.

A camera to watch over you and guide you and call you when what you've done is just swell.

There is a cigarette for the two of you.

You buy a grapefruit more intelligently than a sanitary napkin.

Somehow, you feel more important on TWA.

You own the sun with Coppertone.

"We have invented two things which make lying acceptable: advertising and news management."

ABUNDANCE IS A FREE GIFT

Abundance exists when the needs of human beings and other living organisms can be met from the resources available in the environment.

WAR IS THE CONTINUATION OF DIPLOMACY BY OTHER MEANS
Georges Clemenceau

Library of Congress

"The lamps are going out all over Europe. We shall not see them lit again in our lifetime." Edward Viscount Grey of Falloden.

If necessary, we should bomb Vietnam back into the Stone Age."

DIPLOMACY IS THE CONTINUATION

OF WAR BY OTHER MEANS

"It is a very good sign when you are through for the day and everyone agrees unanimously to the next meeting at a certain time." Henry Cabot Lodge The New York Times, *January 26, 1969*

"I shot a teen-ager; I shot a teen-ager." National Guardsman at Kent State

"The greatest guarantee against the emergence of a police state in this society is the presence of a strong, respected, competent, just police force," Richard M. Nixon, May 28, 1969

"Well, maybe we do need something of the police state; maybe we do need a little repression." Civic leader of El Dorado, Kansas, Time, June 22, 1970

"When the gentlest cop is the one who beats you on the shins instead of the head, you've got to figure something is wrong." Moderate student at University of California, Santa Barbara

"I just didn't think about it. I just closed my eyes and shot.... Everybody else shot, so I shot." Guardsman at Kent State

Recently there has been a growing movement for local communities and neighborhoods to have control of their own affairs. This movement opposes the bureaucratic tendency toward centralization. The principle involved in this movement is clear and simple: people in local communities are ultimately responsible for their own lives, therefore they are entitled to organize themselves in ways which they find desirable.

Various phrases have come to stand for this movement: local control, community control, decentralization. Most of the activity so far has concerned schools and school districts: for instance, in New York City experiments were carried out in which selected communities ran their own school systems. However, the principle of community control can be extended to other functions of a successful community.

It is here proposed that communities organize their own "green force." People in the green force take over the responsibilities of the police which is the "red force."

The green force carries no weapons. They are trained in manual self-defense. It is their responsibility to ensure that communication lines within a community are kept open and that conflicts are foreseen and dealt with constructively. Their aim is to head off potential turbulence in a community by setting up situations in which real problems can be solved.

The green force is meant to replace the red force or police force. Red forces inevitably create conditions which justify their own existence. Therefore, red forces are increasingly seen as undesirable elements by a true community.

A community which needs a red force should be viewed as a failure because its members did not achieve the necessary levels of cooperation and trust among themselves. On the other hand, a community which maintains a green force should be viewed as a success because its members work together to organize and build up their community.

C. and J. Thums

THE CHARACTERISTICS THAT LEAD TO CRIMINAL
BRING SUCCESS IN BUSINESS.

Arizona Republic

BEHAVIOR MAY BE THE SAME AS THOSE THAT

The New York Times, July 18, 1969

We have met the enemy and them is us. Pogo

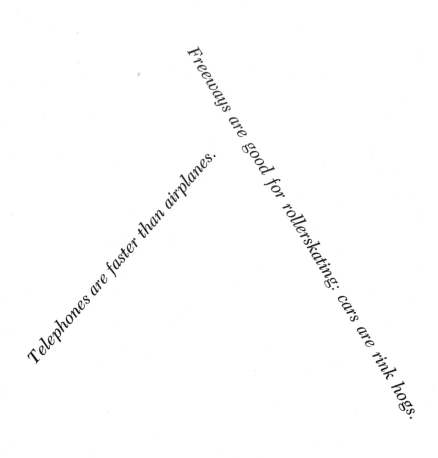

Freeways are good for rollerskating; cars are rink hogs.

Telephones are faster than airplanes.

Poverty is a lack of money.

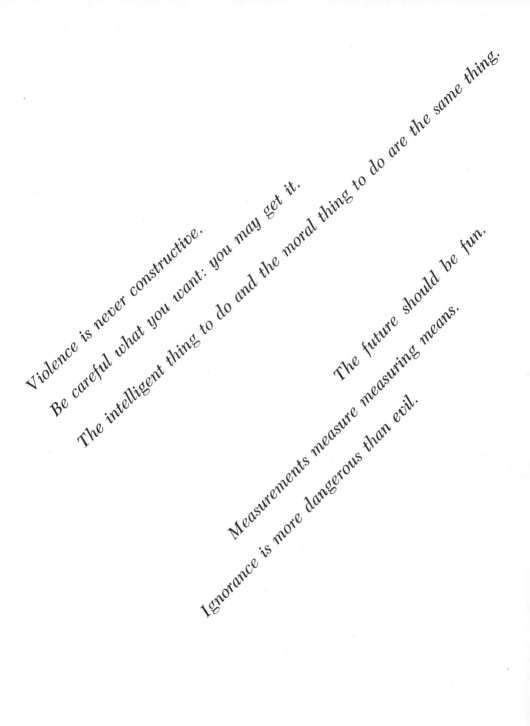

Violence is never constructive.

Be careful what you want: you may get it.

The intelligent thing to do and the moral thing to do are the same thing.

The future should be fun.

Measurements measure measuring means.

Ignorance is more dangerous than evil.

ABUNDANCE IS A FREE GIFT

Excess exists when . . .

No. 1152. Raw Steel Production: 1940 to 1969

[In thousands of short tons. See Historical Statistics, Colonial Times to 1957, series P 203-207, for production in long tons]

YEAR	Total	U.S. as percent of world production	Index, 1957-1959=100	TYPE OF FURNACE			GRADES		Steel for casting
				Open hearth [1]	Electric	Basic oxygen process	Carbon	Alloy and stainless	
1940	66,983	43.2	68.8	65,282	1,700	-	62,017	4,966	
1945	79,702	63.7	82.0	76,245	3,457	-	71,054	8,648	
1950	96,836	46.6	99.7	90,797	6,039	-	86,266	8,570	
1955	117,036	39.4	120.5	108,679	8,050	307	106,376	10,660	
1960	99,282	26.0	101.9	87,557	8,379	3,346	90,862	8,420	
1961	98,014	25.1	100.9	85,383	8,664	3,967	89,338	8,676	
1962	98,328	25.0	101.2	83,762	9,013	5,553	89,160	9,168	
1963	109,261	25.9	112.5	89,797	10,920	8,544	98,714	10,547	
1964	127,076	26.5	130.5	98,956	12,678	15,442	114,442	12,634	
1965	131,462	26.2	135.3	94,779	13,804	22,879	116,651	14,811	
1966	134,101	25.8	138.1	85,303	14,870	33,928	118,732	15,369	
1967	127,213	23.2	131.0	70,690	15,089	41,434	113,190	14,023	
1968	131,462	22.6	135.0	65,836	16,814	48,812	116,269	15,193	
1969	141,262	22.5	145.4	60,894	20,132	60,236	124,832	16,430	

- Represents zero.   [1] Includes bessemer.

Source: American Iron and Steel Institute, Washington, D.C.; Annual Statistical Report. (Copyright.)

No. 1153. Iron and Steel Industry—Summary: 1950 to 1969

ITEM	1950	1955	1960	1965	1966	1967	1968	1969
Steel mill products, apparent supply____1,000 sh. tons__	70,607	81,629	71,531	100,553	99,024	93,667	107,646	102,682
Net shipments___1,000 sh. tons__	72,232	84,717	71,149	92,666	89,995	83,897	91,856	98,877
Exports____1,000 sh. tons__	2,639	4,061	2,977	2,496	1,724	1,685	2,170	5,229
Imports____1,000 sh. tons__	1,014	973	3,359	10,383	10,753	11,455	17,960	14,034
Percent of total supply_____	1.4	1.2	4.7	10.3	10.9	12.2	16.7	13.7
Scrap consumed____1,000 sh. tons__	53,733	63,930	52,106	69,798	70,127	65,422	70,076	76,705
Scrap produced____1,000 sh. tons__	31,006	37,407	33,310	46,682	46,566	43,854	46,679	46,193
Scrap inventory____1,000 sh. tons__	3,845	5,705	7,699	6,005	6,513	6,291	6,808	5,341
Average employment_____1,000__	592	625	572	584	576	555	552	544
Revenues, total_____mil. dol.__	9,534.6	14,049.3	14,221.3	17,971.7	18,288.4	16,880.4	18,679.6	19,566.8
Net income_____mil. dol.__	766.9	1,098.6	810.8	1,069.3	1,075.3	829.8	992.2	850.5
Percent of revenues_____	8.0	7.8	5.7	5.9	5.9	4.9	5.3	4.3
Stockholders' equity____mil. dol.__	5,458.3	7,920.2	10,545.1	12,031.9	12,045.1	12,168.5	12,617.5	13,036.7
Total assets_____mil. dol.__	8,273.0	12,085.8	15,937.4	18,770.9	19,744.6	20,631.9	22,086.6	23,351.5
Inventories_____mil. dol.__	1,384.3	2,090.4	2,990.8	3,228.3	3,616.6	3,740.8	3,561.9	3,811.6
Capital expenditures____mil. dol.__	505.3	713.7	1,520.7	1,822.5	1,952.7	2,145.7	2,307.3	2,079.2

Source: American Iron and Steel Institute, Washington, D.C.; Annual Statistical Report. (Copyright.)

No. 1154. Iron and Steel—Aggregate Exports of Selected Items: 1940 to 1969

[Quantities in thousands of short tons; values in millions of dollars. Includes exports of Puerto Rico to foreign countries. Includes ferromanganese. Excludes steam and hot water heating boilers and radiators. Includes shipments under foreign aid programs; beginning 1950, also includes civilian supply shipments. Beginning 1952, quantity figures exclude, but value figures include, data for wire cloth and other items for which quantities were not reported]

YEAR	Quantity	Value	YEAR	Quantity	Value	YEAR	Quantity	Value
1940	11,876	524	1956	11,574	1,281	1963	9,208	1,048
1945	5,203	461	1957	13,657	1,623	1964	12,051	1,317
1950	3,248	465	1958	6,328	1,046	1965	8,934	1,202
1952	4,854	771	1959	7,009	885	1966	7,763	1,158
1953	3,711	640	1960	11,493	1,187	1967	9,427	1,242
1954	4,826	653	1961	12,442	1,140	1968	8,969	1,227
1955	9,723	979	1962	7,597	947	1969	14,367	1,747

Source: Dept. of Commerce, Bureau of the Census; Foreign Commerce and Navigation of the United States; monthly report, FT 410, U.S. Exports, Schedule B Commodity and Country; Quarterly Summary of Foreign Commerce of the United States; and unpublished data.

Deaths and Death Rates

No. 71. Infant Death Rates—States: 1960 and 1967

[Deaths per 1,000 live births, by place of residence. Represents deaths of infants under 1 year old, exclusive of fetal deaths]

STATE	1960 White	1960 Other races	1967 White	1967 Other races	STATE	1960 White	1960 Other races	1967 White	1967 Other races
United States....	22.9	43.2	19.7	35.9	South Atlantic—Con.				
					West Virginia....	24.8	37.7	24.8	33.1
New England.	21.7	35.2	19.3	33.8	North Carolina....	22.3	52.4	20.0	42.0
Maine..	25.7	12.9	22.8	¹32.1	South Carolina....	23.9	48.5	21.0	37.8
New Hampshire....	23.7	10.6	20.1	¹150.0	Georgia....	24.6	48.1	19.8	39.4
Vermont.	24.2	-	21.0	-	Florida....	23.6	46.1	18.8	37.2
Massachusetts....	21.1	34.4	19.2	34.6					
Rhode Island....	22.4	44.4	18.2	43.5	East South Central....	25.6	48.4	21.8	40.9
Connecticut....	20.0	36.9	17.9	30.9	Kentucky....	26.0	48.3	22.9	36.1
					Tennessee....	25.3	43.5	21.0	36.4
Middle Atlantic....	22.0	41.4	19.2	37.7	Alabama....	24.9	45.0	20.7	38.2
New York....	21.5	41.6	19.1	36.8	Mississippi....	26.6	54.3	22.8	47.4
New Jersey....	21.9	41.7	18.5	38.2					
Pennsylvania....	22.6	40.6	19.9	39.2	West South Central..	24.9	44.3	20.5	35.5
					Arkansas....	22.5	38.7	20.5	34.2
East North Central....	22.1	39.4	19.7	35.6	Louisiana....	22.6	46.9	19.1	37.4
Ohio....	22.2	39.4	19.0	33.8	Oklahoma....	22.7	42.8	19.0	31.3
Indiana....	22.6	37.7	21.0	35.0	Texas....	26.3	43.9	21.0	34.9
Illinois....	22.2	39.6	20.3	36.9					
Michigan....	22.1	40.4	19.8	35.2	Mountain....	25.7	51.7	20.6	33.6
Wisconsin....	21.2	36.3	18.4	36.5	Montana....	24.2	34.5	22.9	33.0
					Idaho....	22.7	33.3	19.5	¹11.0
West North Central..	21.7	42.5	19.2	38.2	Wyoming....	27.5	48.6	23.8	¹8.7
Minnesota....	21.6	22.6	19.5	29.9	Colorado....	26.9	44.0	22.3	33.6
Iowa....	21.7	35.2	18.9	32.4	New Mexico....	30.9	52.8	22.5	37.9
Missouri....	21.4	45.4	19.1	42.1	Arizona....	26.6	60.8	20.2	35.8
North Dakota....	24.1	43.3	21.0	¹21.4	Utah....	18.8	54.0	16.2	¹28.8
South Dakota....	24.2	76.0	20.8	35.3	Nevada....	29.6	33.9	18.6	25.7
Nebraska....	21.3	34.3	19.0	36.2					
Kansas....	21.3	33.4	18.4	34.4	Pacific....	22.6	30.5	18.7	25.0
					Washington....	22.7	36.7	18.3	31.1
South Atlantic....	23.6	47.2	20.0	37.4	Oregon....	23.0	29.2	18.9	32.0
Delaware....	17.8	50.6	15.9	39.3	California....	22.5	29.7	18.8	24.9
Maryland....	22.3	44.6	19.0	32.5	Alaska....	27.9	68.2	19.1	51.2
District of Columbia....	29.4	39.6	20.8	29.7	Hawaii....	21.5	24.0	14.9	17.5
Virginia....	24.6	45.5	20.1	37.4					

- Represents zero. ¹ Based on frequency less than 20.

No. 72. Deaths and Death Rates From Accidents: 1950 to 1967

[Prior to 1960, excludes Alaska and Hawaii]

TYPE OF ACCIDENT	DEATHS 1950	DEATHS 1955	DEATHS 1960	DEATHS 1965	DEATHS 1967	RATE¹ 1950	RATE¹ 1955	RATE¹ 1960	RATE¹ 1965	RATE¹ 1967
All accidents....	91,249	93,443	93,806	108,004	113,169	60.6	56.9	52.3	55.7	57.2
Railway accidents....	2,126	1,344	1,023	962	997	1.4	0.8	0.6	0.5	0.5
Motor-vehicle accidents....	34,763	38,426	38,137	49,163	52,924	23.1	23.4	21.3	25.4	26.7
Traffic....	33,863	37,437	37,142	48,050	51,759	22.5	22.8	20.7	24.8	26.2
Nontraffic....	900	989	995	1,113	1,165	0.6	0.6	0.6	0.6	0.6
Other road-vehicle accidents....	533	330	243	319	288	0.4	0.2	0.1	0.2	0.1
Water-transport accidents....	1,502	1,452	1,478	1,493	1,545	1.0	0.9	0.8	0.8	0.8
Aircraft accidents....	1,436	1,446	1,475	1,529	1,799	1.0	0.9	0.8	0.8	0.9
Accidental poisoning by—										
Solid and liquid substances....	1,584	1,431	1,679	2,110	2,506	1.1	0.9	0.9	1.1	1.3
Gases and vapors....	1,769	1,163	1,253	1,526	1,574	1.2	0.7	0.7	0.8	0.8
Accidental falls....	20,783	20,192	19,023	19,984	20,120	13.8	12.3	10.6	10.3	10.2
Fall from one level to another....	7,117	6,811	6,019	5,802	5,420	4.7	4.1	3.4	3.0	2.7
Fall on the same level....	4,569	4,275	3,689	5,738	5,167	3.0	2.6	2.1	3.0	2.6
Unspecified falls....	9,097	9,106	9,315	8,444	9,533	6.0	5.5	5.2	4.4	4.8
Blow from falling object....	1,613	1,332	1,404	1,493	1,435	1.1	0.8	0.8	0.8	0.7
Accidents caused by—										
Machinery....	1,771	2,019	1,951	2,054	2,055	1.2	1.2	1.1	1.1	1.0
Electric current....	955	1,075	989	1,071	992	0.6	0.7	0.6	0.6	0.5
Fire and explosion, etc....	6,405	6,352	7,645	7,347	7,423	4.3	3.9	4.3	3.8	3.8
Hot substances, etc....	842	742	402	420	376	0.6	0.5	0.2	0.2	0.2
Firearms....	2,174	2,120	2,334	2,344	2,896	1.4	1.3	1.3	1.2	1.5
Inhalation and ingestion of objects....	1,350	1,608	2,397	1,836	1,980	0.9	1.0	1.3	0.9	1.0
Accidental drowning....	4,785	5,046	5,232	5,485	5,724	3.2	3.1	2.9	2.8	2.9
Excessive heat and insulation....	137	615	168	106	96	0.1	0.4	0.1	0.1	(Z)
Complications due to medical procedures....	589	776	1,115	1,494	1,530	0.4	0.5	0.6	0.8	0.8
All other accidents....	6,132	5,974	5,858	7,268	6,909	4.1	3.6	3.3	3.7	3.5

Z Less than 0.05 percent. ¹ Per 100,000 resident population. For 1950 and 1960, based on population enumerated as of Apr. 1; for other years based on population estimated as of July 1.

Source of tables 71 and 72: Dept. of Health, Education, and Welfare, Public Health Service; annual report, Vital Statistics of the United States.

No. 73. Death Rates, 1950 to 1967, and Deaths, 1966 and 1967, From Selected Causes

[Prior to 1960, excludes Alaska and Hawaii. Beginning 1960, causes of death classified according to seventh revision of *International Lists of Diseases and Causes of Death*; see text, p. 45. See also *Historical Statistics, Colonial Times to 1957*, series B 114-128]

CAUSE OF DEATH	DEATHS PER 100,000 POPULATION [1]						DEATHS	
	1950	1955	1960	1965	1966	1967	1966	1967
All causes	963.8	930.4	954.7	943.2	951.3	935.7	1,863,149	1,851,322
Tuberculosis, all forms	22.5	9.1	6.1	4.1	3.9	3.5	7,625	6,901
Syphilis and its sequelae	5.0	2.3	1.6	1.3	1.1	1.2	2,193	2,381
Meningococcal infections	0.6	0.6	0.4	0.5	0.4	0.3	876	636
Acute poliomyelitis	1.3	0.6	0.1	(z)	(z)	(z)	9	16
Infectious hepatitis	0.4	0.5	0.5	0.4	0.4	0.4	757	844
Other infective and parasitic diseases	4.4	3.1	3.2	3.0	3.0	2.8	5,854	5,469
Malignancies	139.8	146.5	149.2	153.5	155.1	157.2	303,736	310,983
Asthma	2.9	3.6	3.0	2.3	2.2	2.1	4,324	4,137
Diabetes mellitus	16.2	15.5	16.7	17.1	17.7	17.7	34,597	35,049
Meningitis, except meningococcal and tuberculous	1.2	1.1	1.3	1.2	1.2	1.0	2,324	2,044
Major cardiovascular-renal diseases	510.8	506.0	521.8	516.4	521.4	511.5	1,021,188	1,012,047
Diseases of cardiovascular system	494.4	496.3	515.1	510.9	516.1	506.5	1,010,812	1,002,111
Vascular lesions affecting central nervous system	104.0	106.0	108.0	103.7	104.6	102.2	204,841	202,184
Diseases of heart	356.8	356.5	369.0	367.4	371.2	364.5	727,082	721,288
Rheumatic fever and chronic rheumatic heart disease	14.8	12.0	10.3	8.0	7.7	7.2	15,012	14,176
Arteriosclerotic heart disease, including coronary disease	213.0	247.0	275.6	288.6	292.7	289.7	573,191	573,183
Nonrheumatic chronic endocarditis and other myocardial degeneration	56.5	39.9	31.8	27.4	27.4	26.6	53,581	52,697
Other diseases of heart	15.9	12.6	14.3	15.1	15.8	15.8	31,042	31,287
Hypertensive heart disease	56.5	45.0	37.0	28.4	27.7	25.3	54,176	49,975
Other hypertensive diseases	8.3	6.8	7.1	6.0	5.8	5.6	11,390	11,181
General arteriosclerosis	20.4	19.8	20.0	19.7	19.9	19.0	38,907	37,504
Other diseases of circulatory system	4.9	7.3	11.0	14.1	14.6	15.1	28,692	29,944
Chronic and unspecified nephritis and other renal sclerosis	16.4	9.6	6.7	5.5	5.3	5.0	10,376	9,936
Influenza and pneumonia [2]	31.3	27.1	37.3	31.9	32.5	28.8	63,615	56,892
Influenza	4.4	1.7	4.4	1.2	1.4	0.7	2,830	1,475
Pneumonia [2]	26.9	25.4	32.9	30.8	31.0	28.0	60,785	55,417
Bronchitis	2.0	1.9	2.4	3.0	3.1	3.2	6,151	6,264
Ulcer of stomach and duodenum	5.5	5.9	6.3	5.4	5.3	5.0	10,321	9,825
Hernia and intestinal obstruction	5.9	5.3	5.1	5.2	5.1	5.0	10,078	9,814
Inflammation of alimentary canal, except diarrhea of newborn	5.1	4.7	4.4	4.1	3.9	3.8	7,552	7,504
Cirrhosis of liver	9.2	10.2	11.3	12.8	13.6	14.1	26,692	27,816
Inflammation of bile ducts and gall bladder, including gall stones	3.9	3.6	2.6	2.4	2.3	2.2	4,592	4,383
Acute nephritis, and nephritis with edema including nephrosis	2.3	1.5	0.9	0.7	0.6	0.5	1,164	1,005
Infections of kidney	2.1	3.0	4.3	5.1	4.8	4.6	9,498	9,006
Hyperplasia of prostate	4.2	3.7	2.5	1.8	1.6	1.6	3,217	3,136
Deliveries and complications of pregnancy, childbirth, and the puerperium	2.0	1.2	0.9	0.6	0.5	0.5	1,049	987
Congenital malformations	12.2	12.5	12.2	10.1	9.3	8.8	18,158	17,325
Certain diseases of early infancy	40.5	39.0	37.4	28.6	26.4	24.4	51,644	48,314
Symptoms, senility, and ill-defined conditions	14.9	12.1	11.4	12.1	12.2	12.2	23,960	24,096
Accidents	60.6	56.9	52.3	55.7	58.0	57.2	113,563	113,169
Motor-vehicle accidents	23.1	23.4	21.3	25.4	27.1	26.7	53,041	52,924
Non-motor-vehicle accidents	37.5	33.5	31.0	30.4	30.9	30.4	60,522	60,245
Accidents in the home	16.0	14.0	13.4	12.4	12.6	12.0	24,771	23,691
Other non-motor-vehicle accidents	21.5	19.5	17.6	17.9	18.3	18.5	35,751	36,554
Suicide	11.4	10.2	10.6	11.1	10.9	10.8	21,281	21,325
Homicide	5.3	4.5	4.7	5.5	5.9	6.8	11,606	13,425
All other causes	40.3	38.3	44.2	47.6	48.8	48.8	95,525	96,533

Z Less than 0.05.

[1] ... population enumerated as of Apr. 1 for 1950 and 1960, and estimated as of July 1 for other years ... [2] Excludes pneumonia of newborn.

Source: Dept. of Health, Education, and Welfare, Public Health Service; annual report, *Vital Statistics of the United States*.

Manufactures

No. **1129.** ALCOHOLIC BEVERAGES—PRODUCTION, STOCKS, AND PER CAPITA CONSUMPTION: 1950 TO 1969

[For years ending June 30. Includes Puerto Rico. Excludes imports. See *Historical Statistics, Colonial Times to 1957*, series P 192, for production of fermented malt liquor]

CLASS	Unit	1950	1955	1960	1965	1968	1969
Beer:							
Breweries operated	Number	407	292	229	197	163	
Production	1,000 bbl.[1]	88,807	89,791	94,548	108,015	117,524	12,...
Tax-paid withdrawals	1,000 bbl.[1]	83,512	84,457	88,929	100,307	107,470	111,...
Stocks on hand, June 30	1,000 bbl.[1]	10,982	11,627	11,458	12,505	13,306	13 1⁄2,
Annual per capita consumption[2]	Gallons	24.99	23.88	24.02	25.46	25.88	...
Domestic	Gallons	24.97	23.83	23.91	25.29	25.72	...
Imported	Gallons	0.02	0.05	0.11	0.17	0.16	...
Distilled spirits:							
Production facilities operated[3]	Number	229	201	178	153	137	
Warehouses operated[4]	Number	309	278	241	268	277	
Production, total[5][6]	1,000 tax gal.[7][8]	208,235	182,142	285,027	206,599	235,388	254,944
Whiskey[5]	1,000 tax gal.[7][8]	118,760	103,927	149,545	117,930	146,702	179,944
Tax-paid withdrawals, total[9]	1,000 tax gal.[7][8]	144,124	153,122	177,952	204,652	227,703	240,34
Whiskey	1,000 tax gal.[7][8]	60,499	74,356	83,589	89,773	96,863	100,3...
Stocks on hand June 30, total[6]	1,000 tax gal.[7][8]	708,562	841,496	931,509	989,794	1,063,460	1,085,9...
Whiskey	1,000 tax gal.[7][8]	643,280	715,861	813,720	841,099	888,106	933,740
Bottled for consumption, total	1,000 wine gal.[10]	161,117	172,304	203,963	244,468	284,543	300,537
Whiskey	1,000 wine gal.[10]	139,653	139,004	146,916	161,385	182,130	188,9...
Annual per capita consumption[2]	Tax gal.[7]	1.48	1.58	1.87	2.13	2.37	2.44
Domestic	Tax gal.[7]	1.33	1.36	1.54	1.66	1.76	1.8...
Imported	Tax gal.[7]	0.15	0.22	0.33	0.47	0.61	0.6...
Still wines:							
Production[11]	1,000 wine gal.[10]	297,857	380,229	511,295	565,055	580,297	611,58...
Tax-paid withdrawals[12]	1,000 wine gal.[10]	135,581	136,279	147,554	162,889	178,440	188,9...
Stocks on hand, June 30[12][13]	1,000 wine gal.[10]	128,433	128,475	142,575	157,010	187,633	180,77...
Annual per capita consumption[2]	Wine gal.[10]	1.33	1.28	1.36	1.44	1.51	1.5...
Domestic	Wine gal.[10]	1.30	1.23	1.28	1.32	1.38	1.44
Imported	Wine gal.[10]	0.03	0.05	0.08	0.12	0.13	0.13
Effervescent wines:[14]							
Production	1,000 wine gal.[10]	1,061	1,716	4,113	6,358	11,282	13,03...
Tax-paid withdrawals	1,000 wine gal.[10]	1,047	1,561	3,296	5,731	9,405	11,26...
Stocks on hand, June 30	1,000 wine gal.[10]	1,619	1,401	2,712	3,616	5,903	6,55...
Annual per capita consumption[2]	Wine gal.[10]	0.01	0.02	0.04	0.06	0.09	0.10
Domestic	Wine gal.[10]	0.01	0.01	0.03	0.05	0.07	0.08
Imported	Wine gal.[10]	(Z)	0.01	0.01	0.01	0.02	0.02

Z Less than 0.01 percent. [1] Barrels of 31 wine gallons (see footnote 10).
[2] Based on Bureau of the Census estimated population 18 years old and over, as of January 1, including Armed Forces abroad. Prior to 1960, excludes Alaska and Hawaii. Source: Dept. of Commerce, Business and Defense Services Administration.
[3] Prior to 1960, represents registered distilleries, fruit distilleries, and industrial alcohol plants. In some instances a plant was operated at different times in more than one of these categories and was counted in each.
[4] Prior to 1960, represents internal revenue bonded warehouses and industrial-alcohol bonded warehouses.
[5] Prior to 1960, net production obtained by deducting total products used in redistillation from gross production of neutral product (spirits); thereafter, each kind of distilled spirits used in redistillation was deducted from gross production of same kind.   [6] Excludes alcohol produced for industrial use.
[7] A tax gallon for spirits of 100 proof or over is equivalent to the proof gallon; for spirits of less than 100 proof, to the wine gallon. (See footnotes 8 and 10.)   [8] A proof gallon is the alcoholic equivalent of a U.S. gallon at 60° F, containing 50 percent of ethyl alcohol by volume.   [9] Includes ethyl alcohol.
[10] A wine gallon is the U.S. gallon, equivalent to the volume of 231 cubic inches.
[11] Production represents total amount removed from fermenters, including distilling material, and beginning 1969, includes increase after fermentation (by amelioration, sweetening, and addition of wine spirits). In 1969, 368,067,164 gallons of distilling materials were produced.
[12] Includes special natural wines.   [13] Excludes distilling materials.
[14] Includes champagne, other effervescent wines, and artificially carbonated wines.

Source: Treasury Dept., Internal Revenue Service (except as noted); annual report, *Alcohol and Tobacco Summary Statistics.*

No. **1130.** DENATURED ALCOHOL: 1950 TO 1969

[For years ending June 30. Excludes Alaska; includes Puerto Rico]

ITEM		1950	1955	1960	1965	1968	1969
Alcohol produced[1]	1,000 proof gal.	313,535	411,840	518,724	658,641	670,071	730,647
Denaturing facilities operated		46	46	38	46	48	50
Specially denatured alcohol:							
Dealers operating		35	35	43	43	47	44
Users operating		4,176	3,939	3,599	3,564	3,418	3,279
Ethyl alcohol used for denaturation[2]	1,000 proof gal.	322,837	395,334	520,512	580,137	542,599	608,947
Denatured alcohol produced, total	1,000 wine gal.	174,674	213,229	279,726	311,778	292,926	326,842
Completely denatured	1,000 wine gal.	4,414	575	679	2,195	2,022	2,229
Specially denatured	1,000 wine gal.	170,260	212,654	279,047	309,583	290,904	324,613

[1] Represents alcohol and spirits, 190 proof and over, produced at distilled spirits plants.
[2] Represents all products (except rum) *used* for denaturation, that is, domestic ethyl alcohol, imported ethyl alcohol, and spirits.

Source: Treasury Dept., Internal Revenue Service; annual report, *Alcohol and Tobacco Summary Statistics.*

Totals in millions of pounds, per capita in pounds. Prior to 1960, excludes Alaska and Hawaii. Per capita figures based on Bureau of the Census population estimates as of July 1, including Armed Forces abroad]

YEAR	COTTON [1] Total	Per capita	WOOL (scoured basis) [2] Total	Per capita	MAN-MADE FIBERS Rayon and acetate [3] Total	Per capita	Non-cellulosic [3] Total	Per capita	FLAX [4] Total	Per capita	SILK [5] Total	Per capita
1930	2,617	21.3	263	2.1	119	1.0	–	–	16	0.13	81	0.65
1935	2,755	21.7	418	3.3	274	2.2	–	–	13	0.10	72	0.57
1940	3,959	30.0	408	3.1	494	3.7	4	(Z)	12	0.09	48	0.36
1945	4,516	32.3	645	4.6	795	5.7	50	0.4	7	0.05	1	0.01
1950	4,683	30.9	635	4.2	1,375	9.1	144	1.0	11	0.07	11	0.07
1955	4,382	26.5	414	2.5	1,455	8.8	448	2.7	8	0.05	11	0.07
1960	4,191	23.2	411	2.3	1,082	6.0	796	4.4	5	0.03	7	0.04
1965	4,477	23.0	387	2.0	1,593	8.2	2,017	10.4	8	0.04	6	0.03
1966	4,631	23.5	370	1.9	1,623	9.6	2,369	12.0	10	0.05	5	0.02
1967	4,423	22.2	313	1.6	1,520	7.6	2,716	13.6	8	0.04	3	0.01
1968	4,147	20.6	330	1.6	1,711	8.5	3,585	17.8	8	0.04	4	0.02
1969(prel.)	3,926	19.3	314	1.5	1,624	8.0	3,913	19.3	5	0.02	2	0.01

- Represents zero.   Z Less than 0.05.

[1] Reported by Bureau of the Census. For American cotton, tare as reported by Crop Reporting Board deducted. For foreign cotton, 15 pounds deducted (20 pounds beginning August 1968).

[2] Reported by Bureau of the Census. Beginning 1950, excludes consumption in cotton and other spinning systems and consumption in batting and felt manufacture.

[3] From *Textile Organon*. Represents domestic shipments plus imports for consumption. Includes textile glass-fiber. Beginning 1935, includes producers waste consumed at mills.

[4] Through 1950, represents imports for consumption reported by Bureau of the Census plus estimated production reported by (a) Bureau of Plant Industry through 1945 and (b) Portland, Oreg., Office of Agricultural Marketing Service for 1950; beginning 1955, imports for consumption reported by Bureau of the Census.

[5] Compiled from reports of Bureau of the Census. For 1930, general imports less reexports; beginning 1935, imports for consumption.

Source: Dept. of Agriculture, Economic Research Service; unpublished data. (Through 1950, in Dept. of Commerce, Business and Defense Services Administration; *Wool and Man-Made Fibers in the United States*.)

No. 1145. SYNTHETIC ORGANIC CHEMICALS—PRODUCTION AND SALES, BY GROUP: 1960, 1965, AND 1968

[Production and sales in millions of pounds; sales value in millions of dollars. Excludes Alaska and Hawaii]

GROUP	1960 Production	Sales	Sales value	1965 Production	Sales	Sales value	1968 Production	Sales	Sales value
Synthetic organic chemicals	53,952	28,760	6,662	88,864	46,807	9,021	120,368	64,578	11,526
Cyclic	17,818	10,735	3,237	28,229	16,499	3,855	39,406	22,265	6,408
Intermediates	9,602	3,964	622	16,865	7,551	814	25,014	11,328	1,121
Dyes	156	148	192	207	190	292	226	215	370
Synthetic organic pigments	40	33	64	48	38	94	54	46	139
Medicinal chemicals	77	55	521	100	72	321	113	77	363
Flavor and perfume materials	33	26	37	53	45	57	60	50	72
Plastics and resin materials	2,716	2,228	628	4,453	3,690	874	5,899	4,902	1,132
Rubber-processing chemicals	170	130	85	211	166	109	264	199	128
Elastomers (synthetic rubbers)	2,283	1,949	469	2,300	1,898	443	2,563	2,017	172
Plasticizers	445	384	103	799	765	133	985	887	262
Surface-active agents	977	927	147	1,371	877	96	1,500	887	94
Pesticides and related prod	525	455	203	683	582	378	930	723	483
Miscellaneous	793	435	165	1,138	625	245	1,798	903	362
Acyclic	36,134	18,026	3,425	60,635	30,308	5,165	80,962	42,314	6,411
Medicinal chemicals	37	33	35	59	57	41	64	45	42
Flavor and perfume materials	22	21	23	46	43	28	57	59	37
Plastics and resin materials	3,427	3,119	1,025	7,232	6,363	1,631	10,461	9,496	1,783
Rubber-processing chemicals	29	22	16	41	28	14	49	37	17
Elastomers (synthetic rubbers)	669	602	229	1,292	1,143	401	1,705	1,546	525
Plasticizers	157	116	45	274	257	81	346	320	112
Surface-active agents	555	472	131	1,799	821	204	2,289	1,111	223
Pesticides and related prod	122	115	59	195	182	119	263	237	163
Miscellaneous	31,115	13,525	1,861	49,697	21,415	2,645	65,728	28,463	4,050

Source: U.S. Tariff Commission; annual report, *Synthetic Organic Chemicals, U.S. Production and Sales.*

No. 96. Hospital Expense Per Patient Day: 1946 to 1968

[In dollars. Prior to 1960, excludes Alaska and Hawaii. Short-term hospitals have an average patient stay of 30 days or less; long-term, an average stay of longer duration]

YEAR	TOTAL EXPENSE						PAYROLL EXPENSE [2]					
	Total	Non-Federal				Fed-eral	Total	Non-Federal				Fed-eral
		General and special		Men-tal [1]	Tuber-culosis				General and special		Men-tal [1]	Tuber-culosis	
		Short-term	Long-term						Short-term	Long-term			
1946	5.21	9.39	2.97	1.39	4.57	6.14	2.93	4.98	1.64	0.80	2.38	4.06
1950	7.98	15.62	5.39	2.43	7.22	12.77	4.79	8.86	3.32	1.38	4.06	9.35
1955	11.24	23.12	8.06	3.73	10.13	14.60	7.20	14.26	5.36	2.17	6.48	11.63
1960	16.46	32.23	12.82	4.91	13.37	20.11	10.92	20.08	9.01	3.45	8.92	16.34
1961	18.46	34.98	14.49	5.53	14.72	23.34	12.25	21.54	10.12	4.00	9.89	19.15
1962	19.73	36.83	15.10	5.72	15.22	24.97	13.12	22.79	10.62	4.16	10.38	20.42
1963	21.00	38.91	16.57	5.98	15.13	26.28	13.93	24.01	11.61	4.40	10.31	21.58
1964	23.20	41.58	18.91	6.97	15.72	27.17	15.38	25.26	13.21	5.16	10.78	22.38
1965	25.29	44.48	19.79	7.50	17.39	28.67	16.70	27.44	13.96	5.60	12.20	23.12
1966	27.94	48.15	20.59	8.11	19.16	29.69	18.27	29.41	14.39	6.11	13.36	23.96
1967	32.54	54.08	21.45	9.62	21.36	33.04	20.76	32.44	15.10	7.10	14.66	25.35
1968	37.78	61.38	27.00	11.25	25.13	37.97	23.78	36.61	18.58	8.29	17.38	27.48

[1] Includes short-term psychiatric hospitals.
[2] Includes full-time equivalents of part-time personnel; except for 1946 and 1950, excludes residents, interns, and students.

Source: American Hospital Association, Chicago, Ill.; *Hospitals*, Guide Issue. (Copyright.)

Mental Patients

73

No. 98. Patients in Mental Hospitals, Outpatient Psychiatric Clinics, and Institutions for the Mentally Retarded: 1935 to 1968

[In thousands, except rate. As of end of year. Prior to 1960, excludes Alaska, and 1961, Hawaii. Completeness of reporting varies from year to year]

YEAR	Total patients	HOSPITALS FOR MENTAL DISEASES				OUTPATIENT PSYCHIATRIC CLINICS			INSTITUTIONS FOR THE MENTALLY RETARDED		
		Total [1]		Fed-eral [3]	State and county [4]	Total	Non-VA clinics	VA clinics	Total [1]		Pub-lic [6]
		Num-ber	Rate [2]						Num-ber	Rate [2]	
1935	(NA)	422	331	23	389	(NA)	(NA)	(NA)	97	77	93
1940	(NA)	479	364	34	434	(NA)	(NA)	(NA)	105	80	101
1945	(NA)	522	409	45	463	(NA)	(NA)	(NA)	119	94	113
1950	(NA)	580	386	54	513	(NA)	(NA)	(NA)	135	90	128
1955	(NA)	634	390	60	559	(NA)	(NA)	(NA)	151	93	144
1958	(NA)	621	363	62	545	(NA)	(NA)	(NA)	162	94	154
1959	965	611	354	63	542	181	140	41	166	95	158
1960	994	611	343	62	536	211	166	45	172	96	164
1961	1,040	603	333	63	527	263	212	51	174	96	167
1962	1,069	591	322	62	516	296	242	54	182	99	174
1963	1,102	579	311	62	505	339	281	58	184	99	177
1964	1,153	566	299	62	490	400	337	63	187	99	180
1965	1,179	550	287	62	475	436	369	67	193	101	187
1966	1,244	523	270	57	452	524	450	74	197	102	192
1967	*1,295	493	252	53	426	609	530	79	*193	*99	193
1968	*1,361	457	231	48	399	711	627	84	*193	*98	193

NA Not available.
[1] Includes patients in private hospitals or institutions, not shown separately.
[2] Patients per 100,000 population estimated as of July 1. Total population used for 1935; civilian, thereafter.
[3] Includes veterans with mental disorders resident in VA hospitals and, through 1965, all patients in public health service hospitals at Fort Worth, Tex., and Lexington, Ky.
[4] Includes patients in State-operated psychopathic hospitals and, through 1950, in city hospitals.
[5] Includes city institutions through 1945.
[6] Excludes patients in private institutions for the mentally retarded.

Source: Dept. of Health, Education, and Welfare, Public Health Service; *Patients in Mental Institutions; Mental Health Statistics—Current Facility Reports; Annual Statistical Report of Outpatient Psychiatric Clinics; Data on Patients of Outpatient Psychiatric Clinics in the United States; Mental Health Statistics*, Series A; *Veterans with Mental Disorders Resident in Veterans Administration Hospitals*; and unpublished data.

[Prior to 1960, excludes Alaska and Hawaii, except for tuberculosis. Figures should be interpreted with caution. Although reporting in some of these diseases is incomplete, the figures are of value in indicating trends of disease incidence. See *Historical Statistics, Colonial Times to 1957*, series B 275–281, for rates for selected diseases]

DISEASE	1945	1950	1955	1960	1965	1966	1967	1968
Amebiasis	3,412	4,568	3,348	3,424	2,768	2,921	3,157	3,006
Aseptic meningitis	(NA)	(NA)	(NA)	1,593	2,329	3,058	3,082	4,494
Botulism	(NA)	20	16	12	19	9	5	7
Brucellosis (undulant fever)	5,049	3,510	1,444	751	262	262	265	218
Diphtheria	18,675	5,796	1,984	918	164	209	219	260
Encephalitis:								
Primary infectious	} 785	1,135	2,166	2,341	1,722	2,121	1,478	1,781
Post-infectious					981	964	1,060	502
Hepatitis:								
Serum	} (NA)	2,820	31,961	41,666	33,856	1,497	2,458	4,829
Infectious						32,859	38,909	45,893
Leprosy	40	44	75	54	96	109	81	122
Leptospirosis	(NA)	(NA)	24	53	84	72	67	69
Malaria	62,763	2,184	522	72	147	565	2,022	2,317
Measles	146,013	319,124	555,156	441,703	261,904	204,136	62,705	22,231
Meningococcal infections	8,208	3,788	3,455	2,259	3,040	3,381	2,161	2,623
Pertussis (whooping cough)	133,792	120,718	62,786	14,809	6,799	7,717	9,718	4,810
Poliomyelitis, acute	13,624	33,300	28,985	3,190	72	113	41	53
Psittacosis	27	26	334	113	60	50	41	43
Rabies in animals	¹9,928	¹7,901	5,799	3,567	4,574	4,178	4,481	3,591
Rheumatic fever, acute	(NA)	(NA)	(NA)	9,022	4,998	4,472	3,985	3,470
Rubella (German measles)	(NA)	(NA)	(NA)	(NA)	(NA)	46,975	46,888	49,371
Salmonellosis, incl typhoid fever	649	1,233	5,447	6,929	17,161	16,841	18,120	16,514
Shigellosis (bacillary dysentery)	34,943	23,367	13,912	12,487	11,027	11,888	13,474	12,180
Streptococcal sore throat and scarlet fever	185,570	64,494	147,502	315,173	395,168	427,752	453,351	435,013
Tetanus	(NA)	486	462	368	300	235	263	178
Trichinosis	(NA)	327	264	160	199	115	66	77
Tuberculosis, newly reported active cases	(NA)	(NA)	76,245	55,494	49,016	47,767	45,647	42,758
Tularemia	900	927	584	390	264	208	184	186
Typhoid fever	4,211	2,484	1,704	816	454	378	396	395
Typhus fever:								
Flea-borne (endemic-murine)	5,193	685	135	68	28	33	52	36
Tick-borne (Rocky Mountain spotted fever)	472	464	295	204	281	268	305	298
Venereal diseases (civilian cases):								
Gonorrhea	313,363	286,746	236,197	258,933	324,925	351,738	404,836	464,543
Syphilis	351,767	217,558	122,392	122,003	112,842	105,159	102,581	96,271
Other	10,261	8,187	3,913	2,811	2,015	1,294	1,309	1,486

NA Not available. ¹ Figures from Economic Research Service, Dept. of Agriculture.
² Based on reports from States: 37 in 1960, 36 in 1965 and 1966, 38 in 1967, and 37 in 1968.

Source: Dept. of Health, Education, and Welfare, Public Health Service, National Communicable Disease Center, Atlanta, Ga.; *Vital Statistics—Special Reports*, Vol. 37, No. 9, and *Morbidity and Mortality Weekly Report* (annual supplement), Vol. 13, No. 54 and Vol. 17, No. 53.

No. 94. Hospital Use: 1935 to 1968
[Prior to 1960, excludes Alaska and Hawaii. Rates per 1,000 population]

YEAR	GENERAL AND SPECIAL HOSPITALS [1]			MENTAL HOSPITALS, ANNUAL RATE [2]		TUBERCULOSIS HOSPITALS		
	Annual rate [2]		Average length of stay (days)	Admissions	Total days in hospital	Annual rate [2]		Average length of stay (days)
	Admissions	Total days in hospital				Admissions	Total days in hospital	
1935	58.6	882.0	15.0	1.4	1,455.0	0.7	174.2	257.0
1940	74.3	1,019.2	13.7	1.4	1,634.0	0.7	185.3	208.0
1945	120.2	1,986.8	16.5	1.9	1,720.2	0.7	164.7	253.1
1950	109.8	1,165.3	10.6	2.0	1,659.4	0.7	174.7	232.3
1955	125.4	1,237.5	9.9	2.2	1,644.6	0.7	145.9	218.9
1960	136.3	1,264.8	9.3	2.3	1,490.9	0.4	86.0	208.3
1963	145.5	1,328.7	9.1	2.9	1,260.6	0.3	52.4	182.5
1966	145.9	1,386.5	9.5	2.6	1,178.8	0.2	39.9	168.4
1967	145.5	1,439.5	9.9	2.7	1,084.4	0.1	22.6	166.4
1968	145.7	1,437.9	9.9	3.0	1,059.8	0.2	26.8	144.6

¹ Includes all types of hospitals other than mental and tuberculosis.
² Based on Bureau of the Census estimated resident population as of July 1.
Source: 1935–1966, Dept. of Health, Education, and Welfare, Public Health Service; *Health, Education, and Welfare Indicators*. (Computed from data prepared

ABUNDANCE IS A FREE GIFT

The potential for abundance exists because . . .

ENERGY

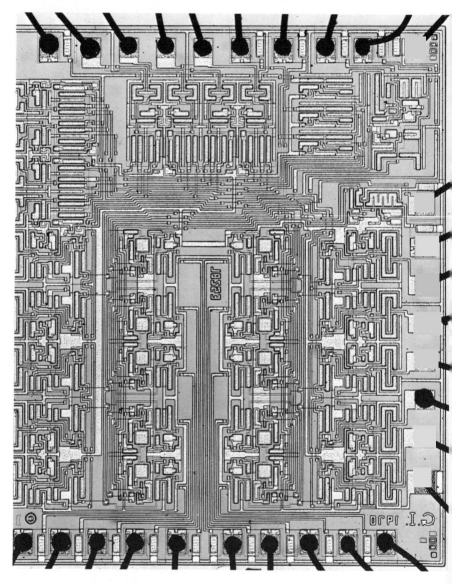

ALCHEMY

Gem Diamonds created by General Electric

Linde Star, a synthetic star sapphire, Union Carbide

Linde Star, a synthetic star sapphire, Union Carbide

EDUCATION

W. B. Nickerson

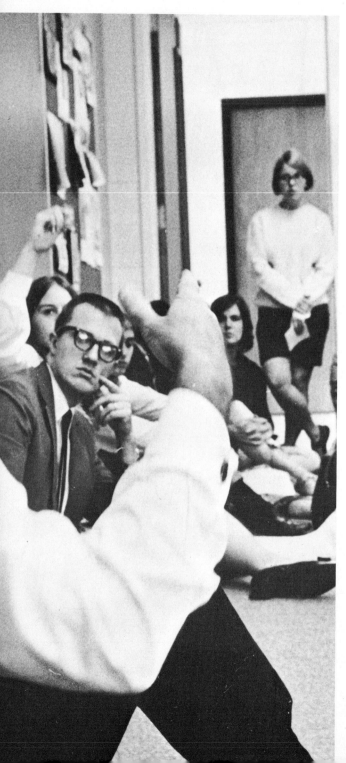

ABUNDANCE IS A FREE GIFT

Abundance exists.

I have sinned against my brother the ass. Saint Francis of Assisi

The superior man is distressed by his want of ability. Confucius

To go beyond is as wrong as to fall short. Confucius

There is endless merit in a man's knowing when to have done. Thomas Carlyle

Rebuke a wise man, and he will love thee. Proverbs 9:8

There is no harm in being sometimes wrong—especially if one is promptly found out. John Maynard Keynes

A man is the origin of his actions. Aristotle

Chiefly the mould of a man's fortune is in his own hands.
Francis Bacon

Man is not the creature of circumstances. Circumstances
are the creature of men. Benjamin Disraeli

He only earns his freedom and existence who daily
conquers them anew. Goethe

Liberty consists in doing what one desires. J. S. Mill

There is one whose rash words are like sword thrusts,
but the tongue of the wise brings healing. Proverbs 12:18.

Volition, O monks, is what I call action. Buddha.

I am very fond of truth, but not at all of martyrdom. Voltaire.

To have faith is not to defy human reason but rather to share divine wisdom. Abraham J. Heschel.

The superior man acts before he speaks and afterward speaks according to his actions. Confucius.

The sage never strives himself for the great, and thereby the great is achieved. Lao-tzu.

The superior man . . . does not set his mind either for anything, or against anything: what is right he will follow. Confucius.

The way of Heaven has no favorites.
It is always with the good man. Lao-tzu.

*He who possesses virtue in abundance
may be compared to an infant. Lao-tzu.*

*Until you become as little children
you shall not enter the Kingdom of Heaven. Jesus.*

As soon as you trust yourself you will know how to live. Goethe.

The future is something which everyone reaches at the rate of sixty minutes an hour, whatever he does, whoever he is. C. S. Lewis

O God, whose service is perfect freedom . . . Book of Common Prayer.

Better one's own duty, though imperfect,
than another's duty well performed. Bhagavad Gita.

Life can only be understood backwards;
but it must be lived forwards. Kierkegaard.

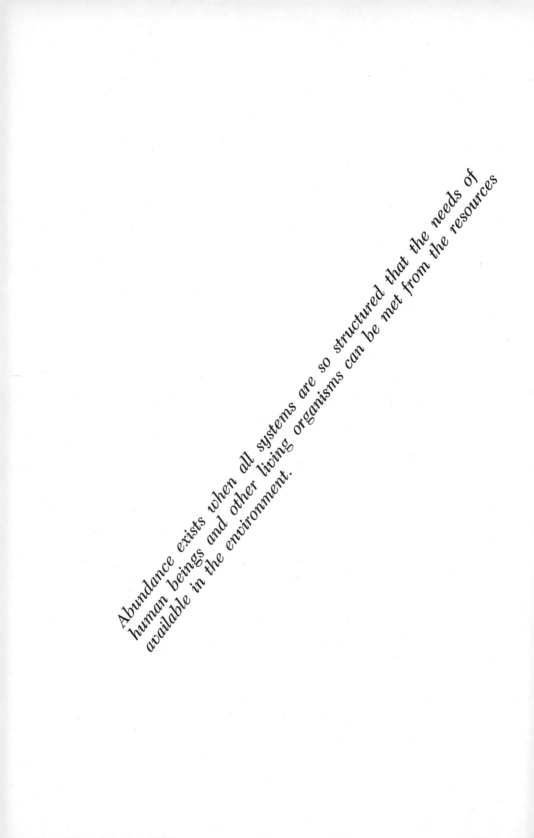

Abundance exists when all systems are so structured that the needs of human beings and other living organisms can be met from the resources available in the environment.

The next pages contain a brief bibliography. It is intended to help the reader find material for further use.

The bibliography has been organized subjectively. It reflects the ideas the author uses in his work. The titles are arranged from beginning to end in what he considers a pattern of developing difficulty. Therefore, you should start anywhere you like on the list and proceed at a pace which suits you.

Future Shock, Alvin Toffler. Toffler notes the increasing speed of social changes in recent years and talks about the possible effects on man and culture. He argues that we have yet to reach the high point of the industrial era.

The Year 2000, Herman Kahn and Anthony Wiener. This book claims to be about the future. Its method is to extrapolate from past trends into the future. Therefore, it shows what the future will be like if it is a larger version of the past.

Player Piano, Kurt Vonnegut. This book explores some logical conclusions of the Protestant work ethic: what can we expect in present circumstances if we apply the idea that each person must hold a job?

The Dialogue Series, Robert Theobald, ed., Bobbs Merrill, pub. The following titles are in the series: **Dialogue on Poverty**, **Dialogue on Education**, **Dialogue on Women**, **Dialogue on Violence**, **Dialogue on Technology**, **Dialogue on Science**, **Dialogue on Youth**. These books were put together to provide material in important problem/possibility areas and to facilitate meaningful dialogue.

Let the Fire Fall, Kate Wilhelm. The author uses a science-fiction setting to talk about events that are occurring now.

The Human Use of Human Beings, Norbert Weiner. Weiner examines some of the moral implications of man's technological advances.

I, Robot, Isaac Asimov. This book relates a series of short episodes about the first robots in the solar system. They change, make mistakes, and become more human.

Politics of Experience, R. D. Laing. Laing takes a second look at people who are labeled insane and placed in asylums. He asks whether some of them can teach us.

Education Automation, R. Buckminster Fuller. Fuller takes a look at what education could be if some present possibilities were actualized.

"An Interview with Warren Bennis," **Psychology Today**, February 1970. A well-known organizational theorist discusses his discovery that the organizational modes of the industrial era won't work any longer.

An Alternative Future for America, II, Robert Theobald. The present situation is the starting point for this book. An overall framework is developed that makes it possible to examine the trends in American society.

I Ching (or **Book of Changes**). This book contains much of the knowledge of old China. It is to be consulted as an old friend.

Economics of Abundance, Robert Theobald. This volume argues that traditional concepts of economics are no longer effective. Unless there is fundamental rethinking of economic realities, increasing levels of inflation and unemployment will plague us through the seventies.

Foundation, Foundation and Empire, Second Foundation, Isaac Asimov. A classic science trilogy. The First Galactic Empire has fallen. A great scientist has devised a plan to decrease the duration of the inevitable period of chaos before the coming of the Second Galactic Empire.

Gutenberg Galaxy, Understanding Media, The Medium Is the Massage, Marshall McLuhan. McLuhan shows how the industrial era fractured man and forced him into linear thinking. McLuhan then discovers what he believes are trails leading toward a new world that promises a more human future.

Operators Manual for Spaceship Earth, Utopia or Oblivion, R. Buckminster Fuller. Unconceivable abundance for all mankind or unlimited catastrophe. These are the choices the author sees for mankind in the next decade. In these books Fuller develops his concepts of how mankind might achieve the first of the two alternatives.

The Technological Society, Jacques Ellul. Ellul shows what the industrial era has done to man and will continue to do until man decides to control his own destiny.

The Book, Allan Watts. Western thinking is in terms of either/or. Eastern thinking is in terms of both/and. Watts talks about Eastern thinking and its impact on human identity.

Toward a Psychology of Being, Abraham Maslow. Maslow breaks with the long-standing trend in psychology of concentrating on pathology. He attempts to develop a psychology for healthy human beings.

Childhood's End, Arthur C. Clark. All the children on earth begin to change in strange ways. The human race has grown up.

Stranger in a Strange Land, Robert Heinlein. Valentine Michael Smith is a human, born and raised on Mars. He comes back to earth and begins to learn what it means to be human.

"Synergy," by Ruth Benedict, in **Psychology Today,**
June 1970. Ruth Benedict originally used the
word "synergy" to describe the attributes of
cultures that were nonviolent. Her work has opened
the way for current thinking about a good
society and how it might be achieved.

The Step to Man, John Platt. Platt is generally
known as a scientist. In this volume he applies
the knowledge of science to current social realities.

Teg's 1994: An Anticipation of the Near Future,
Robert Theobald and J. M. Scott. A story about a
girl, Teg, who wins an Orwell Fellowship in
1994. The fellowship enables her to discover the
significance of developments over the past
twenty-five years and the directions in which
further changes are required.

**The Teachings of Don Juan: A Yaqui Way of
Knowledge**, Carlos Castaneda. This book explores
the world of a Yaqui wise man.

**Phenomenon of Man, Hymn of the Universe,
Future of Man**, Pierre Teilhard de Chardin. Teilhard
develops a new world view. Through his thinking
we can see the world on an evolutionary journey,
developing increasingly more complex physical
forms and increasingly higher levels of
consciousness.

What the Buddha Taught, Walpola Rahula. A
simple, straightforward look at the teachings of
the Buddha. The reader is left on his own to
consider how these thoughts might relate to him.

Expanded Cinema, Gene Youngblood. This book
moves our thinking beyond the linear mode of
existing art. An unintentional mixing of communication styles often obscures the author's meaning.
Nonetheless, this material stems from a truly
fundamental rethinking of "art" and "reality."

ABUNDANCE IS A FREE GIFT

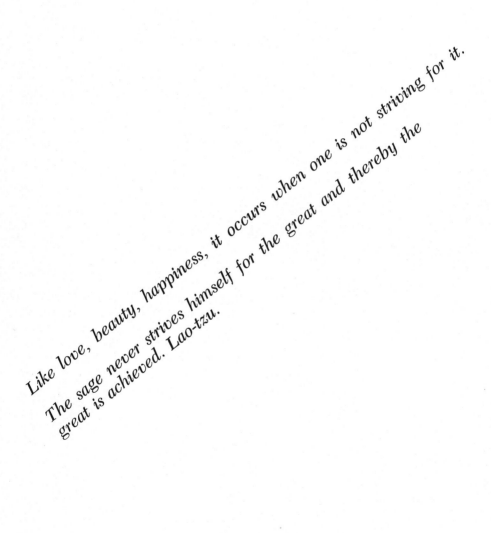

Like love, beauty, happiness, it occurs when one is not striving for it. The sage never strives himself for the great and thereby the great is achieved. Lao-tzu.

Nothing is ever wasted.
Everything is always wasted.

Consider a problem solved when it solves itself.

Style is content.

Process is input.

Time is the interface of space.

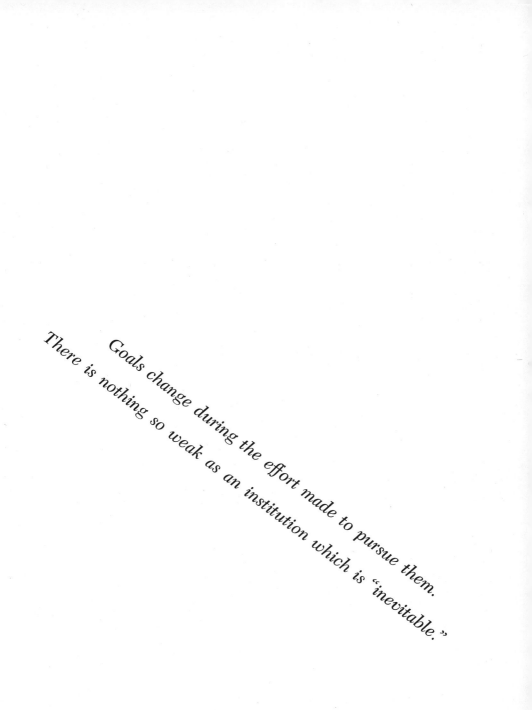

Goals change during the effort made to pursue them. There is nothing so weak as an institution which is "inevitable."

I can only teach you what you already know.

What you find profound is what you don't understand.

A person only learns what he wants to learn.

Intelligence is the only unlimited natural resource.

It is as blessed to receive as to give.

What you know can teach you what you don't know.

NASA

NASA

MAN IS A WORLD PROBLEM SOLVER

NASA

NASA

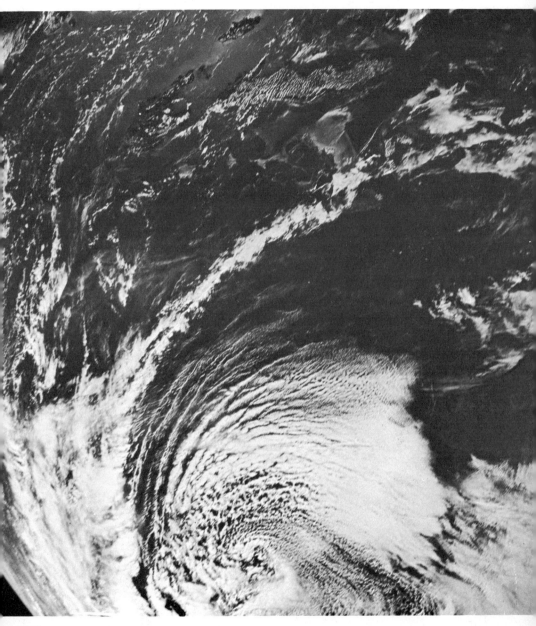

NASA

C. and J. Thums

9 *THE NEED FOR NEW POLICIES*

In the previous chapters we have tried to suggest the new world view required to live in the communications era. In this chapter we shall state the policy implications which stem directly from this new world view.

We shall examine three major topics in this chapter: New Forms of Income Distributions, Aid to the Scarcity Regions, and How to Control Population Growth. These are, of course, only a few of the areas where critical decisions must be made in coming decades. These three have been chosen because they make it possible to illustrate some key decision-making principles. A full discussion of the overall issue of effective decision making lies, however, beyond the scope of this volume.

New forms of income distribution

We inherited our present forms of income distribution from the industrial era. They were well adapted to moving us from scarcity to excess at a time when man possessed limited power. However, they are only appropriate in the scarcity-excess continuum and only so long as man had to be forced to work. Present methods of income distribution are inappropriate and dangerous when men must learn to relate on the basis of sapiential authority.

Today's system of distributing income is, of course, based on jobholding. The vast majority of the population can only expect to be able to live well if they can find and hold a job. Given the realities of cybernation, which will ensure that machines become more effective than men in a wide range of occupations, we must find a new principle for income distribution. However, the urgency of the problems in this area is so great that we do not have time to invent a new principle: we must adapt and develop an existing principle.

This principle must provide an overall *system* for distributing income. We require a pattern which will ensure that *all* those in the culture are able to obtain the resources needed to live in dignity. It is not enough in present circumstances to create new subsystems to solve the problem of those who cannot find jobs in the industrial system: we would then still be forced to preserve an income distribution system based on jobholding. This, in turn, would condemn us to live in a "whirling-dervish economy dependent on compulsive consumption."

Contrary to general opinion, we already have the basis for a new system of income distribution: we can call this basis the insurance principle. In an insurance system, the right to an income does not depend on the ability to find or hold a job but rather on the situation of the individual. People with certain characteristics—youth, age, sickness, unemployment—are entitled to funds on the basis of these characteristics.

The insurance principle has a long history. Even in the most expansive period of the industrial era, people were not willing to rely entirely on the job principle for income distribution. They took steps to ensure help if they should fall sick, should lose their job, or if one of their family should die. Originally, the groups involved in such insurance patterns were small and private. Later, there was a rapid growth of large marketives which insured against an ever wider range of possible risks. Today, the individual who falls sick obtains funds to cover the costs of his illness, and these funds are paid, in effect, by those who remain well. Similarly, those who are working pay funds to the old who have retired; those who suffer losses by fire and theft are paid by those who do not, etc.

Private insurance is however, inherently limited. Quite apart from the problems of growing carelessness, growing fraud, and huge damage awards, certain types of risks cannot be covered without government participation. Movement to the government level was therefore inevitable if the risks of certain citizens were to be covered. So long as insurance systems are carried on by marketives which must make a profit, those most in need of insurance—the poor—will be unable to obtain enough insurance to meet their real needs.

The pressures which have emerged to force change in insurance systems are easily shown in the case of Social Security. During the depression of the thirties, it became clear that many old people had not been able to accumulate sufficient resources to live dignified lives after their retirement. A contributory, compulsory Social Security scheme was therefore set up. It was expected that the amounts paid into the fund and the amount taken out of it would balance. It was believed that the payments to contributors could be based on the amount they had put into the fund. Inevitably, however, the payments made to those who had held low-paying jobs during their lifetimes were totally inadequate.

Various pressures have since emerged which have ensured that the sums paid out under Social Security far exceed the entitlements based on payments to the fund and accrued interest. More and more of the funds are therefore being obtained from general revenues.

The first pressure resulted from the fact that a substantial number of people reached the age of retirement without having paid enough into Social Security to be entitled to a full pension. As even maximum entitlements have never been high enough to permit an individual to live with decency, there has been a trend toward linking entitlements to age rather than to contributions.

Second, when the incomes of the old are based on their past payments into Social Security, a constantly growing economy forces their standards of living behind that of the people who are still working. Social Security payments do not take account of the productivity increases which are normal in Western economies: payments therefore fall even further behind wages in relative terms unless entitlements are continuously raised. The decrease in the relative standard of living of the old is increasingly recognized as unjust, for it was their past effort which ensures our ability to increase the availability of resources at the present time. A true insurance pattern for the old therefore necessarily involves the payment of more money than their actuarial entitlements.

Third, because Social Security benefits have been increased in an attempt to ensure just payments which will permit the individual to live with dignity after retirement, the cost has risen dramatically. The contribution of each individual to his eventual pension has become a larger and larger share of his present income. Today's costs of Social Security are so high that they are heavily undermining the progressive principle which is meant to be built into Western tax structures in order to ensure that the rich pay a larger percentage of income in taxes than do the poor—in actual fact the very poor pay higher taxes today than the middle-class and many of the rich. Political realities and considerations of social justice are now combining to create doubts about the wisdom of raising Social Security taxes further. Any short fall would have to be made up out of general revenues. (The specific evolution discussed in the last few paragraphs is based on American experience; parallel developments have, however, occurred in all the countries in the abundance regions.)

The insurance principle is already basic to Western society. There are insurance schemes against unemployment, against sickness, against old age, against theft, to cover market losses, etc. Even tax systems incorporate the insurance principle to a limited extent, for the amount of money paid in taxes is reduced if certain types of loss are encountered by the taxpayer.

However, this does not mean that an insurance *system* has been created. In order to create a system we must extend the insurance principle to cover all human beings. We must ensure that every human being receives funds as a basic right. *The right to an income must be absolute and not be subordinated to any other criterion*: above all, an individual must not be forced to seek a job in order to obtain this payment.

It was proposed in *Free Men and Free Markets* that this right should be called Basic Economic Security. This proposed right must be carefully differentiated from the policies put forward by President Nixon, whose proposed welfare reforms continue to be based on the requirement that the individual should make himself available for a job. Nixon's proposals continue to require subordination to the job principle.

The primary objection to Basic Economic Security (BES) has so far been that it cannot be effective because people who have the opportunity to obtain an income without work will certainly goof off. This volume has made it clear, however, that organizations cannot continue to be based on structural authority and on positive and negative sanctions. Therefore we must today permit people to do what they believe is important. The insurance principle is the only way to ensure that people can pursue those activities which seem critically important to them. In many cases these activities will be the most challenging and therefore the most important to the society.

As always the reactions to new potentials for freedom will vary. We should accept the insurance principle because of the new potentials it creates, but we must not forget the reality that some will waste their time. How should we handle this problem? In the early days of the industrial era, those who were lazy or unlucky often starved to death or, at best, lived in utmost penury. We salved our consciences with private charity, because we were not prepared to look at the systematic problem of poverty and also because we did not have the resources to eliminate it. Today, we have decided that nobody should starve to death. Unless we wish to reverse this stand, we must move in one of two directions. We must either provide each individual seeking employment with a job which provides an adequate income, or we must provide everybody with an adequate income directly through the development of the insurance principle.

Because of our past history, it naturally appears more logical to continue to provide jobs for all, but there are major traps along this route. The experience of the sixties shows that the retraining schemes designed to make everybody job worthy are not effective. Government retraining is only successful when it takes the best of the unemployed workers— who would often be able to find jobs on their own. The record has been dismal when attempts have been made to work with the hard-core unemployed. While it is certainly true that techniques and methods of training and retraining could be improved, there is no apparent possibility that any dramatic breakthroughs can be expected.

Given the failure of retraining policies, it is increasingly proposed that the government should accept the responsibility to serve as the employer of last resort. Under this plan, any individual who cannot find employment elsewhere would have the right to go to the government for a job. The proposal is clearly based on a parallel with the WPA of the thirties. In the thirties, people who could not find work were employed by the government in activities considered socially desirable. Those who lived through the thirties found the results of much WPA activity highly attractive.

We have examined this pattern a sufficient number of times in this book to recognize that the parallel is faulty. The government could not effectively take on the responsibility of serving as employer of last resort even in today's conditions. The expected continued evolution of automation and cybernation would raise the costs of such a measure to impossible levels over coming decades. More and more bureaucrats would be required to watch over more and more unemployables doing more and more meaningless tasks. The end result of such a direction has been brilliantly depicted in nightmare terms by Kurt Vonnegut in his book *Player Piano*.

The proposal for the development of an insurance principle, which is the only available alternative, appears highly attractive in comparison. Each individual would be entitled to a basic income as a matter of right. The income would be paid on an automatic basis using computers. The income could not be removed under any circumstances.

As we have already seen, it is obvious that a certain proportion of the population would goof off. They would take their money and do nothing. How can we be sure that such a reaction would not be so pervasive as to ruin the country? First, most people are not naturally idle, particularly in the United States. When questioned about BES, individuals state that they themselves would not goof off although they do fear everybody else would do so. It is significant that a large percentage of retired military officers, who receive good pensions at relatively early ages, look for new occupations rather than do nothing.

In addition, the self-actualizing person will naturally be more effective under BES than when he works at a job. The self-actualizing individual knows what he should be doing and, if provided with resources, will take responsibility without supervision. Freeing people with initiative is the major way in which we can dramatically, and rapidly, increase the amount of intelligent decision making about the problem/possibilities facing us.

Second, those individuals who decide to goof off permanently will be the laziest, and often the most inefficient, members of the society. In today's conditions, forcing such people to work actually decreases the effectiveness of the total society. They take up the time of supervisory personnel who could be more effectively used in other roles, and they cause expensive errors. It seems probable that the degree of waste would be less today if we provided an income to those who didn't want to work and ceased to force them into jobs where they are resentful and feel the right to be destructive. The adoption of BES would cut at the heart of the neo-Luddite revolt which we have seen to be so dangerous.

In addition, we might well ask why we only worry about the goof-offs among the poor, when, in the words of a banker who supports the idea of BES: "There are two per cent of bums in *all* income classes." The classic answer, of course, is that the rich only waste their own money while the poor are using funds derived from payment of taxes. Such a view is quite inappropriate, for the tax loopholes accorded to the rich raise the taxes of others just as significantly as the incomes provided to the poor.

Finally, it should be remembered that BES will be introduced at a level which will involve financial sacrifice for those who choose to take advantage of the program. The level of entitlements under BES can be changed in the light of experience. If the problem of goofing off did prove to be critical, the level of income available from BES could be kept sufficiently low that people would continue to find the higher incomes from jobs attractive. (The possibility of lowering the level of BES is included here not because it is a likely consequence of the introduction of BES but to show that the consequences of introducing BES can be controlled.)

The basic problem at the present time is not that people lack competence—or at least the ability to achieve competence. Rather they lack motivation. Job training and literacy training fail today, because people do not believe that any real purpose will be served by putting effort into them. BES would provide people with money; that money would provide the motivation to find ways to improve one's condition: a hungry man can only see the need for his next meal, but the man who is assured of food will start to search for a more satisfactory future. We can confidently expect that the amount of effective work done will increase with the introduction of BES.

Committed spending

In recent years there has been a rapid increase in understanding the necessity of BES. If this were the only step required to create an effective insurance system, we might move toward such a system in the relatively near future. Unfortunately, however, there is another major issue which has so far been largely ignored and which has consequently become dangerously urgent.

The computer and cybernation do not only remove the jobs of the blue-collar worker and the office clerk. They also eliminate jobs of managers and engineers, architects and bankers. The computer is a method of carrying through any task whose nature is completely understood, and where human judgment is not an important element in the process. We can therefore expect to see a large number of people who have been earning relatively high salaries lose their jobs. This process started in 1970. There was a significant loss of existing jobs in engineering and middle management and several other fields. If we are to develop policies in this area, we must first decide whether the society has any particular responsibility to those who lose well-paying jobs or whether such people should be expected to look after themselves.

It would seem that we must develop a supplementary insurance scheme to deal with the loss of a job by people who have received large incomes for a significant period of time. The scheme could be called Committed Spending (CS) to symbolize the fact that some people are committed to certain types of spending patterns and cannot change them immediately.

Income rights from CS would be based on levels of income declared for tax purposes over a period of years. If income fell below a specified percentage of the income earned during the relevant years, the government would make up the difference.

The rights would again be based on the insurance principle and would therefore be absolute. It would not be necessary for the individual to prove that he was unable to find a job. As in the case of BES, rates for CS would be set at rates which would minimize social disruption.

It should be particularly noted that entitlements to CS would be seen as a supplement to BES and would be limited in time. Income entitlements based on CS would decline each year until the individual's income fell to BES levels. The scheme would provide a temporary—not a permanent—cushion.

There are four reasons why we must develop a supplementary insurance scheme. The first is economic viability, the second, personal justice, the third, political stability, and the fourth is the need to open up creative possibilities.

The first reason is economic viability. The expenditures of the people who would be entitled to CS are important to the present structuring of the economy. There is no doubt, of course, about the urgency of changing present expenditure patterns away from ecological destruction, but it remains true that this must be achieved in an evolutionary rather than an abrupt manner. The middle class has indeed committed itself to certain types of expenditures. The expectation of these expenditures continuing is built into the economy and the society, and their rapid elimination would certainly lead to serious breakdowns.

For example, a large number of the educational institutions in America today are in serious financial straits. The withdrawal of a significant number of students because their parents' financial situation became critical might well tip the balance for many schools. The consequent closing of campuses would help to destroy present educational patterns before we have devised new ones more relevant for the communications era.

In addition, it seems clear that one of the major factors holding back the economy at this time is that the middle class is uncertain about its future. Middle-income individuals who have felt perfectly secure for many years are suddenly doubtful about their future and prefer to save money rather than to spend it. If this trend remains unchecked, it could be a key contributing factor to a major depression.

The second reason for introducing CS is personal justice. There can be no provable case here so long as we try to develop the argument using industrial-era concepts. In these terms one can only note that the size of these incomes is largely illusory. They have not permitted large-scale discretionary spending. Rather they have been tied up in an attempt to keep up with the Joneses.

The real question we should ask, in communication-era terms, is whether one is justified in depriving members of a social class of the life-style to which they have become accustomed without giving them time to adjust? We assume that in the communications era the minimum requirement for self-actualization is the satisfaction of man's physiological needs, security needs, and social needs. It is true that the view of middle-income individuals about the extent of their needs is often excessive. However, an understanding that one lives at excessive standards of living must not be forced upon these people through deprivation. Rather they must discover that new patterns can be more satisfactory for them.

The third reason for CS is political stability. It is clear that the creation of a large group of poor, unemployed people who had previously held well-paying jobs would have radically destabilizing consequences. In order to defuse such a threat, which has proved destructive in other countries, it will be essential to introduce an income-maintenance scheme.

We have dealt so far with the negative reasons for adopting CS. The positive reason for CS is the most important—to open up creative possibilities. Just as many people living on BES would find new tasks which they felt capable of pursuing, many of those working at high-level jobs, which they nevertheless find meaningless, would use their CS entitlements to start activities more meaningful to social survival and development. The availability of CS would bring creative people out of advertising, public relations, and other bureaucracies to use their talents for the good of the total society.

The general result of BES and CS should be an unprecedented outbreak of creativity in those areas where creativity is most urgently needed.[1]

The financing of BES and CS

This book shows that over the long run there must be a slowdown in the rate of growth of both population and production. This section is devoted to showing that this slowdown cannot be the first step in the process of change. Indeed, it seems probable that, if we are to change to an insurance system and *also* to fulfill the minimal needs of the scarcity regions, we shall have to use the productive system *far more effectively* in the next decade.

Realism forces us to recognize that most of those in Western countries are not going to be willing to move toward an insurance system if this will raise the tax burden. There is already a serious tax revolt in the United States and other Western countries—it is therefore naïve to assume that there would be a willingness to accept higher taxes to pay for BES and CS. If, therefore, we are to have any hope of the orderly introduction of BES and CS, it must be within the context of rapid economic growth. At the same time we must aim to teach people that continued rapid economic growth is not a long-run possibility. (In this context, one can look back on the sixties and recognize that a great historical opportunity was missed. Gains in productivity were relatively easily achieved in the early part of the sixties, and the introduction of both BES and CS would have been possible without excessive stress.)

There is a hidden assumption here—the argument is based

---

[1] For a more extensive examination of these topics see *Free Men and Free Markets, The Guaranteed Income,* and *Committed Spending* by Robert Theobald.

on the belief that the introduction of BES and CS must follow from intelligent decision making. This assumption contradicts much past experience where only the development of acute crises has ensured change of the magnitude proposed here.

The old pattern of being pushed into decisions by crises is no longer feasible. So long as the overall situation appeared essentially stable, as was the case in the industrial era, it was possible to permit *parts* of the situation to get out of control, for the total situation appeared—and was—relatively unchanging. Now that the *whole* situation is changing, it is essential that we watch all the processes of change and prevent any of them from getting out of control.

If we fail to control the processes of change, our industrial system will collapse. As we saw in Chapter 3, bureaucracies cannot recognize new difference patterns effectively. The time is already upon us when the number and extent of crises—or new difference patterns—will overwhelm the capacity of bureaucratic systems to handle them. At this point, industrial-era cultures will be destroyed and with them the infrastructure necessary to the development of the communications era.

We must therefore introduce BES and CS before a massive combined economic, social, and political crisis erupts. The achievement of the higher levels of production necessary for the introduction of BES and CS, without causing dangerous increases in pollution, will require far greater sophistication in policy making than we know how to ensure at the present time. We shall have to learn how to control the neo-Luddite revolt with its threat to production. We shall have to manage the consumers revolt which could free resources for those who still desire increased quantities of goods or could force us into a depression.[2]

---

[2] A further examination of these issues is contained in *The Economics of Abundance* by Robert Theobald.

Aid to the scarcity regions

In the latter part of the forties and the early part of the fifties, the abundance regions of the world decided that they had an obligation to provide funds to the scarcity regions. Impressed by the extraordinary success of the Marshall Plan, which ensured that relatively limited amounts of American money brought about a transformation of the European situation in the years after World War II, the abundance regions believed that the same patterns could be expected to develop if funds were provided to the scarcity regions. Despite a long continued period of aid, no rapid transformation has occurred, and it presently appears as if the need for transfers of funds from the abundance regions to the scarcity regions will continue for many decades into the future.

Why did the Marshall Plan have such favorable results while the transfers from the abundance regions to the scarcity regions have had such limited effects? Aid to Europe from the United States was successful because the fundamental mind-set of Americans and Europeans is congruent—there are, of course, significant differences between the continents, but their cultures have much in common. This commonality permitted successful discussion of appropriate levels of aid and essentially nonacrimonious decisions about proper ways to distribute the aid between countries. The Western European countries wanted their productive capacity restored, and they had already developed cultural patterns which made high levels of production possible.

Congruence of world views is an essential condition for successful aid. The patterns of aid giving acceptable to donor countries are inevitably tied in with their culture—it is essentially impossible for them to provide aid outside their cultural norms. If the culture of the receiving country differs from the culture of the donor country, there will be clashes between the giver and the receiver over appropriate patterns of control over aid, over the type of ecofacts which should be supplied by an aid program, and even over what types of behavior are helpful.

One example of a low-level clash between cultures may help to clarify the issue. It is common for business in the scarcity regions to be conducted by means of bribery. This is officially anathema to Western values. The skein of bribery is, however, such an integral part of the pattern of action in many scarcity regions that unwillingness to use the channels created by bribery undermines the aid program so seriously that it will fail to produce the hoped-for results. (The Western anger about bribery is all too often naïve. We forget that the West has adopted its own patterns of influencing buyers: individuals with goods to sell often entertain prospective purchasers lavishly.)

A science-fiction story dramatized the issues involved in foreign aid. Several hundred years from now, the earth went to war with two planets. The earth having won, it invited each planet to send envoys to a conference at which they could work out the terms of a foreign-aid program. The delegates of one planet arrived on time and behaved well. They received large sums of money. The delegate of the other planet arrived late and behaved as a conqueror rather than a suppliant. The negotiators from earth naturally refused to provide him with any funds.

In the short run the aided planet appeared to do well. The foreign-aid experts from earth brought with them earth technology which repaired the ravages of the war. The unaided planet, on the other hand, went through a period of great hardship, and the delegate who had ruined the chances of aid was ostracized. Later, however, it was the unaided planet which moved ahead. Unhampered by an earth science which was alien to them, they invented new techniques which seemed "impossible" to those from earth. After fifty years, the aided planet had lost all its cultural patterns and styles while the unaided planet had become as creative and productive as earth—although its science had moved in different directions.

The moral of this science-fiction story may not appear relevant on earth, because it is believed that the basic characteristics of the human race are the "same." Many Westerners—particularly Americans—believe that there is only one normal pattern for human nature and that this is best expressed in modern Western civilizations. This was the theme of W. W. Rostow's book *The Stages of Economic Growth,* which argued that the scarcity regions needed to pass through the same stages of growth as those which had already occurred in the West and that no other route could lead to development.

Those who have followed this book to this point are aware that Rostow's viewpoint is invalid. There are two different ways of looking at the world at the present time. One world view structures reality in terms of the scarcity-excess dichotomy. The other world view sees the possibility of abundance. We have seen that our survival depends on giving up the scarcity-excess dichotomy and moving into gestalt abundance thinking.

One of the basic failures of the past twenty-five years is that the West, which should itself have been changing toward abundance thinking, has not only failed to move in this direction but has even tried to persuade the scarcity regions to join them in seeing the world in terms of the obsolete Western world view. For example, people of many cultures used to believe that it was wise to reduce their needs to what they could reasonably expect to obtain. They tended to be satisfied with what was available. But as the West has interacted with the scarcity regions, it has tried to introduce new consumer needs as a means of stimulating the growth of the Gross National Product. The Chinese philosophy of yin-yang, with its central concept of balance, is far closer to abundance thinking than the efforts of the West to dominate the earth.

We must recognize that past patterns of aid to the scarcity regions have only too often done more harm than good. Aid has often tended to break up structures which were necessary to the functioning of the receiving culture without putting new institutions in their place. We have measured growth and development in terms of Western values which have little relevance to the realities of the scarcity regions.

The dangers of this situation are shown most clearly in the growing attempt to force all employment and income distribution patterns into the straitjacket of the Western "job." In recent years, those concerned with the scarcity regions have recognized that economic growth will not ensure that everybody can obtain resources. Confronted with this reality, it is being argued that we must provide jobs for all. This is obviously ridiculous at a time when it is ceasing to be possible to provide jobs for all even in the abundance regions.

We seem to have forgotten that it is possible to separate the issue of ensuring maximum efficiency in the production of ecofacts from the issue of the just distribution of the right to these ecofacts. We are so used to the job linkage between production and income distribution that we have so far been unable to perceive the implications of the fact that human beings are less and less needed in conventional productive roles. It is now certain that everybody in the scarcity regions cannot be provided with incomes sufficient to live with dignity on the basis of jobs and that new techniques to distribute resources must therefore be invented. These must, of course, grow out of the current income-distribution techniques and basic beliefs of the various cultures. We must therefore expect the development of a wide range of methods of income distribution.

At this point we reach a dilemma. It is obvious that the scarcity regions cannot generate enough resources unless they are provided with help from the industrialized countries. However, the patterns of help the scarcity regions receive from the industrialized countries will continue to be destructive so long as they make their decisions within the framework of the scarcity-excess dichotomy.

This dilemma is very real. Honest analysis of past aid patterns to the scarcity regions leads to the conclusion that the cultural costs of aid have been extremely high. It remains true, however, that without economic aid there would have been even less growth in the poorer areas of the world, and economic conditions would be even worse than they are today.

The argument of this book provides a framework in which the dilemma can be resolved. Mankind's survival requires that we move into the framework provided by abundance thinking. As the change from the scarcity-excess continuum to abundance thinking develops, the change in thought patterns in the abundance regions will carry over to relations with the rest of the world. The assumptions and patterns on which aid is delivered will begin to change fundamentally. The problems of relations between abundance regions and scarcity regions, therefore, can only be appropriately resolved when people in the abundance regions think their way through to an abundance world view.

There will be another consequence of the change to systemic abundance thinking. In the communications era, which is based on systemic thinking, real diversity is not only possible but essential. We will learn that many different styles of cultures can be successful in showing honesty, responsibility, humility, and love, and that there is no way of ranking systems which truly shows these characteristics. As this insight is internalized, we shall become more tolerant of the present patterns of diversity in the human race and less determined to force everybody into the same mold.

One of the most basic of all human traits has been the division of man into in-groups consisting of friends and allies and out-groups consisting of strangers and enemies. The supportive behavior patterns considered appropriate for in-groups were not extended to strangers or enemies. One of the requirements for the future is that we abolish this distinction. Indeed, we must go further and state that all of creation is kin to man. Unless we can understand man's essential relationship to all creation, he will continue to believe that he has the right to dominate those systems which do not contribute to his immediate satisfaction.

This new level of insight must not degenerate into a conservationist stance which demands the preservation of all species at all costs. There should always be a bias toward the preservation of the adaptive potential of all organisms, but other requirements will be more important on many occasions. Species have developed and have died out throughout the world's history. The process cannot and should not be arrested.

Is there, in fact, any way to evaluate the utility and value of various societies. Ruth Benedict, an anthropologist, provided the tools to answer this question several decades ago by developing the concept of cultural synergy. She argued that a society was highly synergetic when it was so ordered that the goals and ideals of the individuals within the society were kept in dynamic balance with the needs and patternings of the whole society. Societies are synergetic when the actions people wish to take and the actions necessary for the society are congruent and not divergent. Conversely societies have low levels of synergy when the desires of those in the society and the needs of the total society clash.

Within the communications era societies with high synergy —and therefore patterns of sapiential authority—are definitionally more desirable than those with low synergy. In societies with high synergy, individuals are permitted and encouraged to do what they wish. In societies with low synergy, individuals find that their wishes are always being interfered with by the norms and the necessities of the society. We can therefore expect that mankind will aim increasingly to create societies with high synergy. Mankind must also come to realize that different types of culture will effectively create synergy in different parts of the world.

As the abundance regions move away from the scarcity-excess dichotomy toward abundance thinking, they will be able to create aid patterns which are more congruent with the real needs of the rest of the world. The countries which are still largely in the agricultural era will find new routes for development which will permit them to move directly into the communications era without passing through the industrial era. The scarcity regions will be able to short-circuit many of the most unpleasant processes by which the abundance regions have reached their present potential for production.

It seems possible indeed that the scarcity regions may find it easier to move into the communications era than will the abundance regions. It is, of course, clear that both sets of countries will have to make profound changes in values and institutions. Nevertheless it seems that the value systems required for the communications era may be more nearly approximated at the present time in many scarcity regions than in the abundance regions. We have seen that the communications era requires an understanding of cooperation and process. These values are essential for the agricultural era but have been largely destroyed in the industrial era.

We have become accustomed to the relative failure of the scarcity regions in past decades. But there is no certainty that this pattern will continue. If it should not, the rapid shift in patterns of success and failure could have major destabilizing consequences. We must, in particular, anticipate a rapid switch in patterns of self-understanding and self-confidence. Already we have seen serious self-doubt emerge in America. The confusions inherent in the shift from the industrial era to the communications era will necessarily add to it.

One specific illustration of coming changes may be useful. The abundance regions presently see themselves as far more developed than the scarcity regions. They base their convictions of superiority on statistics of Gross National Product and income per head. For example, the United States has an income per head forty times as great as that of some of the poorest countries. This justification for feelings of superiority will be destroyed in the near future, for we shall come to realize that economic statistics are unreliable indicators of development.

Economic statistics are unreliable for several reasons. First, economic statistics exclude the work of women in the home. If the value of their production were included, the economic gap between the scarcity regions and abundance regions would narrow substantially. Second, the value of *all* production is counted in income figures: economists value not only useful production but also those ecofacts which are required to get rid of the pollution caused by useful production. It is obvious that deductions for negative production would be far greater in the abundance regions than in the scarcity regions. In addition, it is, of course, unreasonable to measure differences between countries on the basis of economic data alone. It is necessary to examine social patterns and to determine relative success in various social areas. The gap between welfare in the abundance regions and scarcity regions would narrow still further if social patterns were appropriately measured.

How to control population growth

It sometimes appears as though the problem/possibility of the appropriate population size for the human race has been totally confused. One wonders whether we shall succeed in creating a framework in which individuals and societies will be able to make intelligent decisions about how many children they would wish to have. Today some advocate an immediate stop to any population growth. On the other hand, the Food and Agriculture Organization states that the world can feed several billion additional people. Some claim that the way to deal with sickness is to freeze people until the cure for their disease is discovered regardless of the population problem. Others argue that the human race will have to create a new human right which will permit an individual to die when he no longer feels capable of living a meaningful life.

The confusion stems largely from the intense partisanship

of those promoting various causes. Those who are convinced that it is immediately necessary to limit population growth suppress—or at least downplay—data which contradicts their case: thus the advocates of immediate population control have continuously denigrated the significance of the Green Revolution which could make it possible to feed a far larger population than was previously thought feasible. Those concerned with promoting agriculture continue to suppress—or at least downplay—the findings which show that human beings need more than food, clothing, and shelter to survive and that overcrowding is itself dangerous to mental and physical health. They also ignore the real possibility that the Green Revolution may fail.

We shall not begin to discover the real situation until we look at all the evidence honestly. There is no longer any place in our society for groups which use public-relations techniques to advance a specific cause. Our only hope is that we all begin to search intensively for the route into the future which will ensure the survival of the human race. We must lay aside the preconceptions which prevent an unbiased search for the current realities.

What range of populations would be desirable in the world? We can ignore for purposes of this discussion those who refuse to admit that upper and lower limits to a desirable population size exist. Present population growth will lead to standing room only on the earth. We can therefore assume that there is an upper limit to a desirable world population: the reality of a lower limit is also clear, although less relevant.

The restraints on population size in this context are not the absolute ones set by the need for production of minimal levels of food, clothing, and shelter. Rather they are related to the physiological and psychological needs of human organisms for appropriate amounts of space. It is clear that these limits are partially set by cultures, but they are also determined by basic built-in human patterns and reflexes. There has been too little study of human beings to know these limits as yet, but intensive work done with rats suggests certain results which may be relevant for human beings. Studies show that

■ as population densities rise, infant and maternal mortality rates increase dramatically but not enough to prevent further increases in density. There is an effective end to normal parental care, accompanied by undernourishment and cannibalism. It should be noted that these results cannot be related to a lack of food since enough is provided for the growing population. The significant variable is population densities, and the studies show that beyond a certain point increases in density cause increases in antisocial behavior.

■ in high-density conditions, males differentiate into three main groups: a hyperaggressive group, recluses, and homosexuals. The pecking order of male dominance changes with far greater frequency than in normal conditions and more vicious behavior results.

■ normal feeding, rest, and activity patterns decay and are replaced with patterns which cause undernourishment, lack of rest, and various forms of antisocial activity.

■ if the overcrowding occurs in one cage in an interlinked series, the pathological effects are felt throughout the system, for the animals in the uncrowded areas do not know how to protect themselves.

■ if animals are later removed to more usual conditions, many of them prove incapable of reverting to previous behavior patterns.

The parallels with conditions in the inner cities are so obvious that we dare not ignore them. We must begin to plan on the basis of the fact that there is a desirable upper limit to population density and that this has already been reached in many parts of the world.

The overall population density in America is low—the high densities in certain limited areas result in large part from social policies which have forced people to move to the cities. (As we have seen welfare policies, among others, have this result.) A redistribution of population between regions in the United States would create acceptable density levels and leave room for immigration. On the other hand, there are many parts of the world where outmigration will certainly be required if population densities are to return to acceptable levels.

We have not yet done enough work to discover the limits which are set by man's need for space. We have even less knowledge at the present time of the amount of resources we can draw from the environment or the limits of recycling techniques. But whatever these may be, it is clear that the chances presently are very high that world population will grow beyond the optimum point and that the population of many regions will be far above acceptable levels. This is true because the combination of continuing high population growth rates throughout the world and the potential for further medical breakthroughs together ensure that even the largest possible effort will not prevent a very large increase in the present population of the world.

It is this recognition which all too often leads to fanaticism among those concerned with population growth. They recognize the high probability that population growth will continue until it exceeds desirable levels, and they argue that the human race should create laws to limit the number of children people are permitted to have. For example, it has been suggested that a birth control agent should be introduced into the water around the world and that those who wished to have babies would have to go to the clinic to get an antidote.

It would be fascinating to chronicle the peripheral aspects of such a proposal: for example, the effect on other species, the dangers of a black market in licenses and babies etc. However, it is necessary to concentrate on the main issue. Those who suggest mandatory birth control believe that it is possible to force people to behave in ways which are repugnant to them without setting up disastrous feedback patterns.

We have already recognized that we must move toward a society based on sapiential authority. We must create a society in which individuals have the competence to obtain the knowledge required to make intelligent decisions about those issues which confront them. The right to determine the number of children in a family is—and for the foreseeable future will be—one of the most critical decisions open to individuals. The use of structural authority in this area of decision making would therefore be peculiarly inappropriate.

If we were to employ structural authority, we would be forced to set up rules. For example, we could state that every female would be entitled to bear two children—obviously the limitation would have to be on female parents and not male. We would then be forced to determine whether a woman has to be married in order to have the right to bear children. We would have to decide whether women who did not bear children had a right to dispose of their rights to children. Or would we be prepared to force women to bear an unwanted child? We would have to decide how to deal with women who did conceive a third child. There is no end to the problems we should have to solve if we should move in this direction.

It might be suggested that children should only be born in test-tubes as suggested in many science-fiction stories. However, it seems fairly clear that few of the social problems inherent in rearing children would be solved by this approach and that many new ones would be created.

As an alternative we could set up a structural-authority system based on the qualifications of the parents. We would then have to determine either what qualifications were required to permit an individual to have a child or what defects were sufficiently serious to eliminate the right of an individual to bear a child. The reality of recessionary genes which do not appear in each generation would require the creation of a full life history of both partners. It would also require the creation of a profile of "desired" characteristics if decisions about the right to have children were to be effectively made.

There is no need, presumably, to argue the case further. The use of structural authority to control population could only create the most disastrous consequences. Decisions about appropriate family size must, therefore, be made by those directly concerned.

This conclusion, however, does not necessarily imply that the rate of population increase will decline less rapidly than at the present time. Indeed, it seems possible that family size may decline more rapidly once we fully agree that decisions in this matter cannot be coerced.

The number of births in many areas of the world is presently far higher than people desire. There is a large unfulfilled desire for effective and culturally acceptable methods to limit births. Birth rates will therefore decline *if* we satisfy this demand. For example, the abortion issue in the West must be seen in this light. A number of women feel that limitation of births through abortion is acceptable to them. They should be entitled to receive abortions so long as they do not force them on others. There are, of course, religious barriers to this approach. It is argued that abortion and birth control are inherently evil. This viewpoint is unrealistic in the light of the absolute need to control population.

It also contradicts our growing knowledge of the behavior of other species and the natural law. It has hitherto been assumed that species give birth to as many young as is biologically possible. This is incorrect. One example is that many birds limit the number of eggs they lay so that they will have sufficient time and energy to feed all their young. The number of eggs laid by a species will vary with climate and other conditions. Surely mankind is as intelligent as the birds.

If we are to limit the number of children born, one of the methods which will help to reduce the birth rate will be to widen the range of situations in which the individual can relate to children. The nuclear family prevents extensive interactions between older and younger people except in their roles as parents and children. If families and communities were structured in different ways, some people might not want children of their own. In addition, it is clear that there are presently profound social pressures to have a "normal-sized" family: i.e., two or three children. Employers clearly believe that their employees are more likely to be reliable if their families fall within the established norms.

Attempts to meet the wishes of these who want to limit births will require more effort and imagination than we are presently mobilizing. We have a responsibility to set up new social institutions which will make a large family nonessential.

EPILOGUE

In the industrial era, man aimed to learn more and more about less and less. The goal was to become a specialist in a small, clearly defined area of knowledge.

In the communications era, one needs to understand the operation of all the systems which affect one's activities. As one gains knowledge, one recognizes that there is no end to this process.

This book therefore cannot be complete in itself. For example, the policies discussed in the previous chapter are only a small part of the steps which will be required. All that can be done here is to attempt to help others perceive the alterations which are now developing and to deepen their involvement in the process of change.

If this book has been meaningful to you, you will therefore want to learn more. While each person must develop in the directions most relevant to him, nevertheless you may find clues to possible steps in Chapter 8, both in its material and its bibliography.

Books are normally objective media which convey little of the concerns of the author. This volume is inherently subjective. If you have reached this point, you will have learned a great deal about what I value and what I hope man can achieve. It therefore seems appropriate to end this book by wishing you success in your own personal route toward development.

STANFORD ERICKSEN

Robert Theobald is one of the most important socio-economic path-breakers of our time. While studying economics at Cambridge and Harvard, Mr. Theobald became convinced that our present economic assumptions are incorrect and that they are leading us toward global breakdown. His discussion of this theory at campuses throughout the United States led to the writing of HABIT AND HABITAT.

Mr. Theobald developed the theories of guaranteed income and income maintenance for those who lose their jobs due to automation and cybernation. His works include *The Challenge of Abundance, Free Men and Free Markets, The Guaranteed Income, An Alternative Future for America II, Teg's 1994,* and *Futures Conditional.*

A reader, gardener, and rider, Mr. Theobald lives with his wife in Wickenburg, Arizona.